Yo

put the

I got to know Tony's story very well during a project we did together and find it to be one of the most remarkable spiritual transformation stories ever. Not only is it different to any other conversion story that I know, but it is honest, real, gritty and life-changing. I recommend this book and it is my prayer that people all over the world would read it and learn more about the wonderful love of God

—**FRANS CRONJE** IS A SOUTH AFRICAN FORMER CRICKETER WHO PLAYED FOR BORDER, GRIQUALAND WEST AND ORANGE FREE STATE DURING THE 1980S AND 1990S. HE LATER BECAME A FILM PRODUCER, DIRECTOR AND WRITER, SPECIALIZING IN CHRISTIAN FILMS, INCLUDING *FAITH LIKE POTATOES*.

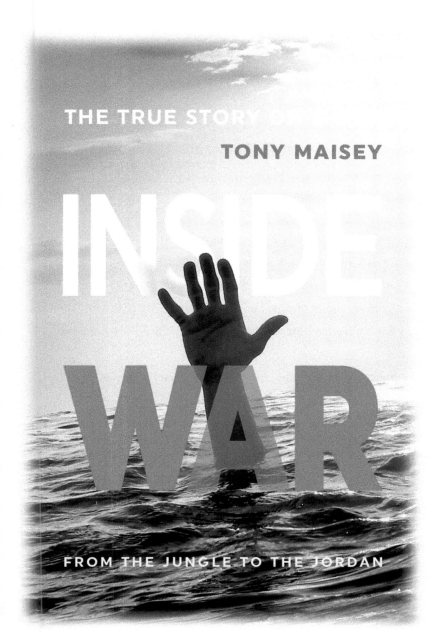

THE TRUE STORY OF

TONY MAISEY

INSIDE

WAR

FROM THE JUNGLE TO THE JORDAN

BRIDGE
LOGOS

Newberry, FL 32669

Bridge-Logos
Newberry, FL 32669

Inside War
From the Jungle to the Jordan
by Tony Maisey

Library of Congress Catalog Card Number: 2021936136

International Standard Book Number: 978-1-61036-266-5

eBook International Standard Book Number: 978-0-7684-6193-0

Hardcover International Standard Book Number: 978-0-7684-6194-7

Large Print International Standard Book Number: 978-0-7684-6195-4

Cover Production and Interior layout by Kent Jensen | knail.com

Cover Design by Cameron Toman

TABLE OF CONTENTS

PROLOGUE

It was a wet wintery morning. Gerry and the Pacemakers' 'You'll Never Walk Alone' was playing on the radio. It was 1976. I clambered up onto the back of my grandparents' sofa to watch the rain hammering against the living room window. A tall slim figure struggled to open the garden gate with one hand while holding a large black umbrella in the other. The gate flew open and then the man headed down the path. A moment later there was a loud knock at the door.

My grandmother came from the kitchen holding a tea towel with wet soapy hands, wearing her usual flowery apron with her sleeves rolled up, continually coughing with a cigarette dangling from her mouth.

'Tony, get down off the sofa with your shoes on', she hollered at me. I jumped down and ran to stand behind her legs. She opened the front door and the Priest stood there in all black wearing a white dog collar. He shook the rain off his umbrella, folding it down. Then he entered the hall with stout authority.

After walking through each room speaking verses of scripture from the Holy Bible, he then concluded that there was an evil spirit in the house, toying with me, the little one.

And so, when I had overheard the grownups talking later that same day, this then confirmed the feelings I had every time I had stayed at my grandparents'. Although I could not see it with my eyes, I had sensed a dark intelligence, a black void in the hallway, just outside my uncle's bedroom door.

I stood at the end of what seemed like a really long hall and watched the man of God open his umbrella and then bid us all a good day. But what my grandparents had failed to mention to him before he walked through the garden gate and then disappeared along the lane, was that they were in regular contact with evil spirits, during their Ouija board séance meetings they held.

So just like the words of Gerry Marsden that came out of my grandmother's radio when the Priest came to visit all those years earlier, it seemed I too would be destined to 'never walk alone.'

CHAPTER ONE

2014—38 YEARS LATER—PERU

The aircraft began to descend over the Andean mountains as I continued to weigh up in my mind whether or not I would return alive from the jungle of Peru. I began to accept my chances were slim. I had broken something deep inside this time, and I knew it would take a miracle to put it right.

And so, in my sickness I went one way in the desperate hope for a cure, in search of a witchdoctor.

Although my life had been a reckless one, living on the edge, seeking the very highs in life had only really been, in essence, to sustain the extreme lows. But never in my life had I been at a point of no return like this before. I needed to find the answer fast or perish far away from everyone I loved.

Like a weak wounded animal, I would just disappear, suffer and die alone. But this jungle medicine, this potion I was now pursuing, had become my only hope of survival, even though the darkness inside continued to whisper—'This time, you've gone too far'.

I'd been existing in denial for many years living many different lives, and I had learned to master the art of hiding the frightened child behind the mask of a fearless lawbreaker. But I was now having to admit I'd finally lost the fight and was struggling to hold up that same old weary disguise. Burnt out without the strength to carry on the lie any longer, I realised I had no choice but to throw the dice one last time offering up my life, in the hope I might win a better one.

In a few minutes I'd be touching down in Lima, Peru's capital, where I would stay one night before taking a two-hour internal flight to Iquitos City, deep in the Peruvian jungle, with no roads leading into it, a place only reached by light aircraft or via a very long boat trip along the Amazon river.

The place was known as the gateway to the jungle lodges and tribal villages.

Other than a few natives returning to their Amazonian homes the small aircraft had been seated with mostly New Age seekers of light and, just as I was, these men and women were flying in to partake in a shamanic ayahuasca ceremony. We were in search of the answer to the same age long question, which is—what's the meaning of life and how do I break free from all its wickedness?

I ventured from bar to bar in downtown Iquitos and each was packed with young handsome people.

I must have appeared to them like a middle-aged desperado as I swayed through the crowd drunk and poisoned on a history that finally had caught up with me. Then I remembered a remark from an old friend. 'No crime goes unpunished son, not one...'

Surely that was it, I was being punished for all I had done.

The top shelf had been my best friend all my life, and so I was about to frequent her once more.

I ordered my usual large brandy, but this time accompanied with a double shot of tequila, to help quicken my escape. Then I asked the barman where the cocaine could be found. 'Hey Chico! This is Peru, right? Make a call', but no one wanted to serve the drunk stranger with their local pearl.

Maybe it was for the best. After all, cocaine only made me paranoid, depraved and sick. I would have gone on to look for a woman of the night in the hope she might fill the gaping hole inside of me, but they never could, it was simply too deep, and they dare not venture in.

I had been a feared man, even an important one, at least in my own foolish eyes, but now I was so very distant from that representation. I had done it all and seen it all and had got my hands on most of it, but it had done me no good, I wasn't a winner, I was a loser, and now it was all over. I'd failed.

I had grown in criminal status from a young teenager, working through the ranks from petty thief to violent knife wielding thug, to armed robber, to the panache of a global drug dealer. But in all of it I only ever sought the answer to the same old question, which was—Who am I?

But in the end, it was all a lie. I was none of those people.

So, it must be true, you really do reap what you sow, I reasoned, and now I had fallen as a consequence of generational crimes, and my own added foolishness. Surely all the lies had finally revealed the absolute truth, which is incapable of telling any lie. And therefore if that same truth represented a sharp double-edged sword, then it had begun carving me up inside like mincemeat.

I stood there surrounded by people but felt the loneliest man that had ever filled two shoes. Even if I wanted to run, I was trapped. I'd been the devil's soldier all my life, and now the tormentor was bent on sending me crazy for wanting to turn away and desert his band. I was in this now, and no one could help me except maybe those witchdoctors out there in the jungle. They were my only hope.

I came around, took my head off the bar and knocked back the shot of tequila I had passed out alongside. Then I paid the check before heading for the door, pushing my way through the crowd out onto a street I didn't remember walking up. The dense Amazon air laid on me heavy, so I leaned against the window to take a few minutes.

I was hungry, but the stench of charcoal-cooked meat wafting on the midnight river breeze did little for my appetite. I walked to the corner of the street passing a skinny dog and lit up another cigarette trying to gauge my drunkenness. My head began to spin so I sat down on a nearby bench to prevent myself from falling. Everywhere seemed so bright, the streetlamps, the colours of people's clothes and the yellow tuk tuks were so vibrant as they whizzed past, reassuring me I was still alive.

I laid my head down and must have fallen asleep sometime shortly after midnight...

I had been in Iquitos some four or five days and had spoken to many natives attempting to find the best lead on where to go to get well. They all offered up one tribe and said they knew the best shaman and would take me there by boat. All I had to go on was my gut and it kept telling me No! Don't go that way and No! This guy's not sound either. I began to search out the gringos in the hope we might have something in common, even if it was just the colour of our skin.

All I needed was to be led to the right tribe where the odds might be stacked in my favour of survival and a safe return back to Iquitos. I was beginning to hear more and more horror stories of people not returning after taking the potion, tales of people losing control and the witchdoctors losing their calm. It was becoming common knowledge that some were going missing and not coming back out of the jungle alive. Stories of lone female seekers being raped while under the influence of the shamans were regularly told. Then there were the accounts of crazed men running deeper into the jungle away from the tribal village only to be found days later half dead and completely deranged.

I would sit each day outside a small bar on the dockside watching the western light seekers returning from the camps, some looked distraught, some relieved and some I just couldn't tell.

I would try to get close to get a better reading of what was really going on out there. They all seemed to have this glazed look of bewilderment in their eyes and there was an air of silent emptiness about their souls as if I was witnessing defiled soldiers returning from the battlefield.

There was an unspoken knowledge that filled the dockside and I couldn't tell if it was a wisdom I wanted. But I had to at least try and dig a little deeper, so I leaned in to get a better understanding of what it was they were bringing back out with them. Was it the truth they had found or just a part of the world that still existed where they could be totally lost in something that was hidden largely from the rest of humanity?

Many were looking for the next drug, the next new high, any fix that gave them the chance to venture further away from the reality of the life they knew, and what it had to offer their confused souls which was very little. They searched for a way to stay lost in a world they felt they didn't fit into. I understood this as well as anyone. I too felt all my life like I had been here on planet earth just observing, like a fly on the wall, rather than being a part of society.

I noticed after a while there was a white man that passed the bar quite often, driving a motorcycle taxi. He was the only white tuk tuk driver I'd seen. He pulled up and came in ordering himself a pint of beer. Once we got talking it turned out he was English and had moved to Iquitos some years before, marrying a local Peruvian girl. He said he had originally come from South West London, England, and had lived close to where my eldest daughter had grown up. What's the chances of this I wondered to myself?

I told him I was there in Peru to drink the ayahuasca potion because I had suffered with depression, alcohol and drug addiction. And how I finally in the end attempted to drink myself to death alone in a trailer, on the south coast of England, in a place called Peacehaven.

'Of all the names', I said, 'what an irony. I was at my lowest in a town named Peacehaven, but the mission failed'. I continued, as I downed a double shot of tequila.

I went on to explain how severely I needed help, and if I didn't get it, I had already made my mind up not to return to London, but instead die there in the jungle, like a sick animal. I told him I had spoken to the local Indians, and although desperate, I didn't feel comfortable going with any of them, but I didn't have enough time left to be messed around, as I felt nearly dead already.

He said I was right to be cautious. He then recommended I meet with the Gringo Shaman who lived out of town a little and had a lodge in the jungle and that his blend was potent but that he wasn't a crook. The guy even had the Gringo's number and offered to drive me out to see him. 'Maybe this is the right move', I thought, so I asked him to call the man. The shaman told me he was next drinking his potion on the following Tuesday evening shortly after sunset, just three days away. I told him where I was staying, at La Casona hotel, and he said that he would arrange for a Canadian girl that would be drinking with us to meet me there on the day, so we could travel to out to meet him together. 'You'll know her', he said, 'she has body tattoos'.

It was all arranged, so I celebrated the possibility of surviving this whole thing, by drinking myself into oblivion. I could trust the way I thought on booze. I'd been weaned onto it from very young and so coming from a drinking background it had been a huge part of my culture and therefore a comfort and security wherever I was in the world. I found time, space and even wisdom in the realm of drunkenness which had surely helped me stay interested in a world I struggled to understand. I guess I found my equal in the booze. Even if it was a false friend it kept me company to say the least.

CHAPTER TWO

THE DARK WATCHMAN

Nicky was an attractive girl, around thirty, and she had a kind way about her which made our meeting go easily. While we waited in the garden of La Casona for the Englishman to pick us up, we spoke openly about our personal afflictions and why we were there in the jungle seeking help. She worked in real estate and lived in a lakeside property on the Yukon in the northern territories of Canada. I told her that living close to the wilderness had been one of my many dreams of escapism in the past, so with added interest I listened to her story more intently. This helped to ease the anxiety that loomed over what was about to unfold.

Holding back the tears, she went on to explain how she had lost both her parents in a recent plane crash, and that she needed answers. Sadly, although she hadn't said as much, I could see that Nicky was on a mission to try and make contact with her deceased family.

On the way to meet the shaman, Nicky warned that the potion was very strong and insisted, with kindness, that when he offered me the choice of full or half cup, I should only take half. We arrived at his home near the tiny Iquitos airport, which was a little detached place. Chickens were running around a smoky bonfire, there were wind chimes and a large dreamcatcher hanging from a tree.

He was a nice enough guy, making me feel welcome as he shook my hand, wearing a white, heavily stained wife beater vest and a pair of baggy old ripped jeans as if he'd been working on his truck, but I don't think he had been. He looked haggard, burnt out even, with a leather looking, sun dried face and long strands of stringy grey hair springing out of a high balding forehead. He seemed to be, on first appearance, a poor advert for the healing of the soul, but I was in no position to be picky.

We waited a little while for a third seeker to arrive who would be drinking with us. As the stranger neared the house on foot along the dusty road, I immediately felt wrong about him. He was a tall sleek white man, with a cold pale face and a dark blank look in his eyes. He just seemed awkward, like a poorly trained spy, now out in the field, but not ready for the assignment given to him. Something sinister went with the man, and maybe that's all he needed. A dark watchman assigned the post to mark me then report to the devil himself, I thought.

The three of us got into the Gringo's rusty old Toyota Hilux and headed out to the edge of the jungle, driving down narrow sandy tracks until we came to his timber lodge about an hour later. It was dark when we arrived and there were two Indians waiting inside for us talking under candlelight. I lit a smoke, standing outside, preferring to be alone for as long as possible before it began. I assumed it to be no coincidence, and that there would be some spiritual significance as to why we were about to drink the potion under such a large full moon, but I didn't ask.

There was a long dormitory that housed about 15 beds and we were guided there to pick one each, the watchman and myself, that is. Nicky would stay with the Gringo afterwards at his house.

I wondered if there was more to that, but I think the American was rightly protecting the only western woman in the camp. He didn't know me or the tall guy so we could easily have been a double act having gone there, separate, but with other disturbing plans in mind. So, it made sense and also put me a little more at ease realising the American had some order and foresight about him.

The circular ceremony hut was about 30 metres in diameter and the shaman had a kind of wooden altar at one point on the outer edge of the perimeter that stood higher than the rest of the dry mud floor where we were now seated randomly on basic wooden chairs. The two Indians were sitting on the far side directly opposite us wearing normal everyday clothes, including baseball caps.

They were later joined by a native woman and her young son who was about ten years old.

I asked Nicky if the boy was going to drink the potion and she said yes, he had shown from an early age that he was spiritually gifted and therefore when one is recognised to be in tune with the supernatural he would be taken under the wing of the shaman and trained in the art.

The witchdoctor entered the hut after being gone for some while. He was now wearing a white robe with different shamanic symbols hanging on black lace around his neck. His long wiry hair was now tied loosely back in a ponytail. He sat at his high position and began chanting something in an ancient tongue, pouring the dark liquid from a clay container into small wooden vessels each a little larger than a regular egg cup. He then drank a cupful, before walking to the natives, who sat obediently, each waiting to receive their dose.

The Indians began to make deep, long burping noises from across the dimly lit hut. I had no idea what was happening. Then

Nicky passed me a wooden bowl and said, 'You might need this to be sick in later, not everyone vomits, but most do'. She then turned away and began to burp herself. I asked her what was going on, 'What's all this burping about?' I asked as they all got louder.

She stopped and answered. 'It's basically purging, clearing negative energy away', she explained lighting up a mapacho cigarette and passing it to me. 'Here, smoke this', she said with a warm smile. I took it and tried to relax, drawing on the strong smoke. I turned to my left to see why the dark watchman wasn't purging, but he was just sat there silent, with his eyes closed as if meditating.

I tried burping, but couldn't get into it, so I gave up, glancing along to Nicky, thankful for her guidance anyway.

The shaman moved towards us and stopped in front of Nicky.

'Half or full cup?' he asked her.

'Half', she replied, glancing up at him with a childlike look of submission in her eyes, trusting he held the answers to her eternal questions. She then turned to me and nodded with another generous smile. I knew what she was saying. Try half first. You can always take more a couple of hours later.

He turned his attention to me.

'Half or full cup?' he said, in the same monotone.

'Half', I replied.

He then moved to the dark watchman.

'Half or full cup?' The man opened one eye and replied 'Full', then closed it again as the shaman turned and slowly hovered across the hut, back to the altar, his cloak floating behind. He poured the measures for us and a minute later returned and passed them slowly one by one.

I peered into mine before drinking. It was dark green, almost black in colour with a strong, earthy odour. I looked to Nicky for more guidance, this being her second visit to Peru and her third ceremony with the Gringo. I thought if she's come back for more it must be OK, so I swallowed it.

'Now I'm in', I thought. 'Even if I wanted out, and tried to vomit this stuff up, it's too late. Some would still be in there'. It was a vile, bitter, salty taste that I had to work hard at holding down.

I turned again to Nicky. 'Have a good trip', she said reassuringly, as she downed her measure in one, screwing her face up at the horrid taste and silky texture. 'You too, have a good one', I replied, trying to look like I wasn't nervous, also feeling the sickliness in my gut as the potion worked its way down through the inner parts, hoping I wasn't going to bring it all back up.

I turned to the imposter hoping he wasn't going to freak me out halfway in.

'Have a good evening,' he said without any honest conviction of heart, his eyes still closed. 'You don't know what you're in for' he followed up with, then I caught him open that same eye and look across my back to Nicky. I spotted the beginnings of a snide smirk developing in one corner of his mouth, just a slight twitch. The smirk of the jester unable to conceal the mocking spirit that lived inside. That same hyena I had trained myself to sniff out so well, navigating the paranoid, drug induced lunacy of the criminal underworld that had been a part of my whole life.

'What are you laughing at, pal?', I snarled and spat out, giving him my evil eye, the look I had successfully used to terminate the plans of so many would-be liberty takers in the past. He never said a word and didn't even acknowledge me. He just sat there, remarkably calm and unnerved with his eyes shut. I realised I was heading completely down the wrong street, so I consciously pulled back the reins and bit down, refusing to be pulled into wrong thoughts that could possibly trigger a psychedelic car crash up ahead.

Nicky touched my hand softly. I turned away from the dark watchman and looked at her.

'It's OK, he means you're going to enjoy it', she said, a little worried that maybe I was going to be the problem, the one to freak us all. I turned to him again, his eyes now open and I forced a smile, 'Enjoy your trip', I said, then turned away and stared down at the cracks in the dry mud that were just recognisable by the flickering of the randomly placed candles around the hut, and just waited in silence.

I wasn't wearing a watch, but I had been told the potion generally took 20 minutes to kick in.

I guess after that I lost all track of time and reality as I had always known it to be. The shaman continued to chant an icaros, occasionally stopping suddenly, then I would notice how the wild jungle noises outside had been silenced also.

I had no knowledge of the spiritual implications of what I had landed myself into. The spirit of the anaconda was something these people worshiped, though I had little understanding at the time. I was just so in need of help and didn't much care where it came from. But then this thing came up through my body as I held my head in my hands. The head of a large snake filled my palms.

My skull had now changed shape into a reptile. Then it retreated back down repeating the same motion over and over again. I had wilfully, but unwittingly, given it permission to enter me, and it was taking full advantage.

All I could sense from the watchman's direction was darkness, like a hole full of thick black tar. It was the same as that void in the corner of my uncle's bedroom all those years before as a child. It just kept going deeper and darker and thicker.

The man didn't speak a word the whole time. He never purged or vomited once. I was convinced he was there just to witness my terror and then report back his findings. My jailer wasn't going to let me go free that easily. I could not move from the chair. I was stuck there. At one point I saw Nicky was on the floor, curled in a ball, crying out to her parents, but I could not help her. I could not move although I desperately tried. I was glued down.

I blinked and then the Gringo was there chanting something over her, hovering. Then he began to laugh out loud, looking up holding out his hands. I now wanted to vomit because of his demented cries. I was still gripping the wooden bowl as I began to open my mouth, but nothing would come out, then a long unhuman groan released from deep inside of me, but it sounded like it had come up from the depths of the earth.

'Get out!' I gurgled. Then all went quiet again. Now it seemed as if every bird in the jungle this time had gone still and silent, paying homage to the forces of darkness at work. Then the thing inside began roaring louder, in some violent dispute I had no say in. I tried to roar it out, but it just wouldn't detach from me.

I opened my eyes and looked down. Nicky's face turned to me looking up from the ground

'What is that thing?' was all she could muster, then she turned back to the earth and continued to wail into the cracked mud in search of her dead parents. And I still could do nothing for her.

I was completely overpowered. It was as if hell itself was accessing the hut directly through me.

The shaman continued to chant and laugh, but he was not helping anything. All the time the dark watchman was just there silently marking me. I eventually managed to lean forward, and I fell off the chair onto the ground, letting go of the bowl, curling up in a ball alongside Nicky.

Now whenever I closed my eyes, I saw the image of what light seekers had called the female spirit of the ayahuasca plant standing pregnant, surrounded by unhuman faces, beckoning me to go deeper, further in, and to then circle around her body.

But I pulled back every time, searching for any hint of a reality I knew and could trust, attempting to lock onto anything in the hut, a person, a doorway, a shard of moonlight, a piece of mud that I could recognise to be from planet earth, but the faces continued to torment. Some at times resembled humans but were clearly not.

I was desperate for it to be over and to return to some kind of normality. At times it felt like it was lifting, and I was returning, but then it would draw me back into a deep, dark, suffocating wave and I would be spinning out of control once more, under its full force. It lasted for 5 hours by all accounts, when finally, I could open and close my eyes for any sustained time, and I knew I was in normal reality, time and space and was free from its grip. Somehow, I had survived it and I was returning back to myself, but in what shape, I had no idea.

Once everyone returned from the realms of darkness, we began to slowly stir and mix around the hut. I remembered at some point the shaman came to us individually and put something oily on our foreheads on the top of our scalps and down our spines at certain points. Then we were free to go outside and were told, ironically, we would be safe from evil spirits.

Not once did I hear a murmur come from that young Indian boy in the hut. I was shocked his parents could send him into such horrific realms at that young and tender age.

We tried to explain what we had experienced individually, as we sat under a tree. But I was finding it difficult, I just felt shattered, so I just stared up at the large moon grateful that I was back in reasonable control. The jungle noises had resumed, the animals had gone back to their usual business. All seemed well. I walked to the dormitory shortly after and got into my chosen bed and covered myself, attempting to hide behind my mosquito net.

I was fragile and still seeing kaleidoscopes of different colours. I just needed rest and eventually fell asleep.

I was gently awoken by one of the Indians around 8am. 'Everyone has gone. I can give you a lift on my bike to the Gringo's home, if you would like. You will not find your way out of here very easily alone', he kindly whispered. I sat up and looked for the imposter, but there was no sign of him. His bed neatly made, he had left. I was the only one there. I stood up and agreed to take the lift.

The breeze on the back of the motorbike felt good and helped wake me up. At some point, it must have rained in the night, I held on tight to the Indian's waist as he navigated the wet, red clay tracks, until we reached hard road. I had a sense he was sent to look out for me, and I was grateful to be experiencing daylight. To see local kids waving to us as we rode by and vehicles passing on the opposite side helped to stabilise my thoughts and nervous system. I still was feeling very emotional.

We got back to the Gringo's, place and as I got off the bike, I thanked the Indian. He held my arm and simply said, 'Protect yourself and be careful who you drink with.' He then broke his grip, turned the front wheel and rode away. I knocked on the door and the American invited me inside and made coffee.

Nicky was still upstairs in bed and I couldn't work out if they had been together. The thought made me strangely feel a little jealous. I felt a little protective of her. She had lost two people that she loved very much and was desperate for answers. I would have liked to have laid alongside her and just held her tight all night, nothing more. I needed that too.

She eventually came down showered, holding her rucksack. 'I've got to get my shit together, my flight is at 11.30, I've got half an hour before I need to be there!'.

I agreed to go with her to the airport.

She was crying most of the way and I tried to console her, holding back my own emotion from the whole ordeal. We got to the airport and sat outside smoking jungle tobacco, talking some more until she had to leave. I was starting to get a feeling of loss, even though I had only known the girl for less than twenty-four hours. We had travelled to strange places together and I still didn't know if that had been a bad or a good thing. Only time would tell.

We hugged and I was sorry to watch her pass through departures out of sight, crying as she went.

I walked to the motorbike taxi rank and got into the first one. 'La Casona, my friend', I said to the driver, looking back one last time as we pulled away, hoping she would somehow get a handle on her life and pull through.

CHAPTER THREE

A HOPE TO KEEP ME GOING...

I limped into the reception of the hotel La Casona, trying to hold back an avalanche of emotion that I had accumulated over three decades. All that self control had been undermined by the events of the night before. I knew if it slipped, the whole mountainside would give way. I stood there, exhausted from the weight of it all, as I lingered patiently for the young man to pass my room key from the pigeonhole.

I made my way through the little courtyard which housed a few tables and chairs standing among a proud blaze of flower beds, where large blue butterflies the size of my palm had gathered in the garden the previous day, when I had found it a pleasant place to sit and contemplate life with Nicky over some good local coffee and a smoke.

There had been an influx of new arrivals, fresh in, holding a get together in the courtyard. A strong looking bald guy in his late thirties, with a New Zealand accent, seemed to be in charge.

It became clear they were a mixed bunch, having flown in from various parts of the globe and it was a forgone conclusion that they were preparing to go out into the jungle and drink the potion together, the New Zealander clearly being their dependable team leader. I decided I would walk back out of the garden with my eyes down, not wanting to engage for fear of being found out. But just then I was drawn towards a woman who was sitting to the left of the bald guy. I zoomed in. She seemed very nice, giving him her full attention, but then she turned her head towards me, and for only a second, we locked eyes.

I liked her profile, face and neck, but it was the shadowy flash in her eyes that drew me the most. I caught a glimpse of someplace dark and I knew it was very murky down in there. Being always driven by mystery and sensual gratification, instead of it repelling me, I was enchanted.

Right then though, I was like a Coca Cola bottle inside that had been shaken intensely, and the lid was now increasingly working loose. I was about to froth over uncontrollably.

I made it to my room somehow and eventually got the door open, breathing a fleeting sigh of relief as I entered, while at the same time taking in the safety of solitude. I had become more and more accustomed to my own isolation as the years went on after many times of relentless disappointment. But at least I could finally drop my shoulders temporarily, once more.

I had never been a man to cry much, especially about my own stuff in the basement. Fears, guilt and shame I had learned to lock up tight. I had purchased that big fat padlock many years before and secured it to the basement door which only I ever knew the combination to. Never did I share it with anyone, not a soul. Now that same hatch door was rattling like mad. The stuff inside had come alive and was kicking up a stinking riot. I dropped to my knees in that room and broke down and sobbed like a child lost in a cold, dark wood.

I don't know how long I laid there curled up on the cool floor tiles of my hotel room. At some point I fell asleep and in my dreams I somehow made the decision to keep going on into the extremity.

I was now in a kind of no-man's land in a state of limbo. I had taken the potion, but I knew I was far from healed. Where could I go from here, other than drink more of the stuff and delve further on into the unknown, in the hopes of finding a way out? I was not fit to return home to London, that I was sure of. I had a kind of hollow, flat feeling in my gut and the thought of drinking booze wasn't so attractive, which I sort of welcomed for once. Surely, I would just have to keep going.

I sat up and leant my back against the creaky wardrobe. I then heard people speaking in the hotel courtyard just a few yards away, so I began following the shadows of people passing beneath the door. Maybe it's time to find out more about the girl with the darkened soul I thought, plus I needed a coffee and a smoke.

I dragged myself to my feet, ran the cold tap, refreshing my face and cleaning my teeth.

Then I looked in the mirror, closer still, into my pupils. 'You've come this far, now you keep going,' I purposely spoke out loud into the room, needing the reassurance from my own voice that I was indeed still alive. Convinced enough, I opened the door and shuffled out.

I asked if I could join a table where a young white Englishman was sat. But he was one of the party of seekers I had passed in the garden earlier. I ordered a coffee from Reception and then sat down at his table and lit a cigarette. I was amazed at how many

Brits were in Peru searching for a hope that might set them free. He had a glazed look in his eye, one of fear. I knew it well. He was running from something and tired of pretending. I started to feel uneasy about the man, although I couldn't be sure if it was because of the ayahuasca that was still circulating in my blood stream.

I began to weigh up everything with added caution through this new pair of spectacles that were now a fixed addition. It had only been twelve hours since the Gringo's ceremony had wound down and I was still having to take tentative little steps. I was in unchartered territory as I could feel the emotion beginning to stir again. I was having to fight it to the point I thought, 'Maybe the way forward would be to keep letting it out.' But I had no desire to break down in front of anyone else, especially another fella.

The man had a little thin landing strip beard running from his bottom lip down through the centre of his chin which I thought made a man look suspect anyway. So, maybe that was it, I was biased.

We got talking and he began telling me how he had just flown in from Dallas, his journey being an exhausting one, having a long stop-over between his flight into the US from the UK and then find out when he reached Lima hours later, that his luggage had not been transferred between flights. So, he was now having to go into the jungle wearing just the clothes he was standing in.

I was a few smokes in and starting my second coffee when the girl with the darkened soul came prancing down the steps into the garden area. She made a beeline for our table and I scanned her as she drew near. Her eyes were hazel green and she walked with a swagger that told me she knew how to handle herself among men. Maybe she had brothers back home.

I gathered she was in her early forties. She had a strong nose and a good set of teeth. There was a stubborn strength behind a broken smile which indicated she had seen it all and was disorientated with her findings, yet she was still willing to keep searching for the truth, which I liked. She sat down without an invitation and I could see these two were familiar. She drew close to him and I had to assume they were an item. She was a wholesome woman alright, and those eyes without a doubt told a dark story I seemed to be unconsciously lured into.

Originally from the American Midwest she spoke with smooth easy notes that slowly lassoed me in as I continued to listen and weigh her up. She wasn't wearing a wedding ring, but I still sensed she was spoken for and maybe it was even this fella with the landing strip facial hair, which made me question her judgement. But it turned out they had just flown in together from Dallas. Tom and the girl were no more than light seeking traveling companions that were about to embark on the same spiritual endeavour, nothing more. This perked me up a lot because I was attracted to her right from the start and needed something to latch onto, a hope to keep me going.

The New Zealander with the smooth head had a Mediterranean girl with him in her mid-thirties.

She headed our way and sat down at our table. Tom and Stella stood up, saying they were going for dinner somewhere in town and so I curiously watched them leave together and then turned to the Mediterranean to give her my full attention.

The Spanish girl began explaining to me how she had been practising shamanism for some four years, drinking the ayahuasca over seventy times or more. She confirmed what I had already been told, that their party were going into the jungle for two weeks, leaving the following morning to drink with the Shipibo tribe. I was sitting down-wind from her and could smell her scent traveling on the light breeze that passed through the garden. This now painfully began to remind me of how much I still needed to be saved, picked up and held, like some pathetic stray dog.

'So—if its healing you seek then there is a space left on our fast boat leaving tomorrow. You are welcome to join us. You will need to be on the dock for 9am, we leave 9.30 sharp', she said, flicking her thick brown hair away from her flushed face, knocking back her chilled sparkling water, at the same time breaking me out of my childish daydream. I nodded, saying that I needed healing and was interested. She then motioned to Smoothhead who was talking on another table with one of the other group members. He nodded and headed over to us.

I agreed the $2,000 he asked for, without questioning the value of what I was getting. How could he have honestly given me the answer to that impossible question anyway, the value of it all? But I had a good idea that staying with those indigenous tribes out there in the rain forest would have cost very little and nowhere near the money mentioned. Nearly all of it was going straight into his pouch. I couldn't put a price on anything, anymore. I had an ultimatum to make which far outweighed any amount of money I could ever count in a whole lifetime, which was, do I keep going or lay down and die?

I really was on my last legs and I realised I never had the time, strength or wisdom to look elsewhere for help. Anyway, I was starting to seriously doubt if I ever would really get the help I needed. Maybe I had blown some kind of human gasket and the leak was beyond repair. All I knew was this group that were staying in the same hotel as me were leaving tomorrow to go four hours along the river to stay with a tribe and do this murky stuff many times over the scheduled two weeks. And, that they were an organised ready-made family that were offering me the opportunity to go with them. They were my only immediate chance of survival and so I decided I had no choice but to continue.

It didn't look like much of a fast boat as I stepped off the pontoon onto the vessel. It had a small outboard engine with a propeller on the end of a long shaft. It seated comfortably around a dozen or so passengers and had a canopy overhead to keep off the sun. It was a really humid hot day. I had a headache and had been losing fluid heavily, I guess, after passing out on all the booze etc. that was still in my system. So I guzzled back a bottle of mineral water like my life depended on it and the headache lifted.

I had got to know a few of the westerners that made up the group from mixing in the hotel courtyard the day before. It was clear we shared the same desperations. We were seeking out the same answers and had similar wounds that needed healing, I guessed. This gave us a sense of belonging to the same club, of lost misunderstood desperados. Whatever our individual reasons for being on that boat, one thing was for sure, we were all on the same trip now, there would be no mistake about it. At least I had one ceremony under my belt, and so I knew roughly what to expect.

I nodded a hello to them as I stepped on but that was as far as I wanted to go with the niceties. We had a long journey on the Amazon river ahead of us and I wasn't in the mood for talking, but I could see this American kid wasn't going to leave me alone till he knew more about the tattoo on the inside of my forearm and what the words stood for.

'Man, I like the tat, man. Does that say, 'Get busy living or get busy dying?' I nodded to him with a half-smile hoping that would do.

'What does it mean to you, man, to have it etched on your arm bro?' I now had to make an effort in the thick humidity.

'It's from the movie, the Shawshank Redemption. I just always liked the line,' I said, wiping away a puddle of sweat from the base of my neck with my bandana. He nodded his head in some kind of spiritual agreement then turned to speak to another younger guy to his side then he pointed back towards my forearm. I blocked them out and looked down into the water observing the dead fish floating amongst the driftwood.

As the boat was slowly getting loaded, I wondered whether the thing would be stable enough.

I licked my salty top lip, looking away from the sun, realising I needed some water for the trip.

I had itching mosquito bites on my legs that I had drawn blood from scratching them too hard, so I didn't fancy the thought of piranhas shooting straight for me in the event of a capsize. Then there were the crocodiles just waiting for it all to happen.

The heat now was becoming unbearable and my arm nearest the side was getting hotter, so I tried to wedge it down inside of the vessel and make it disappear to prevent any further discomfort. I was beginning to feel a little uninterested and irritated as the passengers continued to load in.

We were packed like sardines and then one of the group declared that he had forgotten something and so we had to wait even longer while he grabbed a motorcycle taxi back to La Casona.

I had to break free and get off the boat for a few minutes to try and cool down. I wanted a cigarette and I thought I should also try and find some water for the trip. The seekers kindly moved out the way as I politely pushed through from the middle of the boat. It felt like I was escaping something nasty. The novelty of cruising down the Amazon was starting to wear thin and the thought crossed my mind to grab my rucksack and just walk away.

Stella was sat at the front and as I pushed through, she held out a small bottle of chilled water. 'Go on, take it. I have a full pack here.' she said.

I thanked her, being genuinely grateful, then walked along the pontoon and lit a smoke.

Although I had no interest in any romance, Stella being on the boat was enough to make me keep going and not throw the towel in and head for the nearest bar, although my stomach still felt a little unsure since the Gringo ceremony. I flicked the cigarette butt into the river, swallowed the last of the water, and with a little bit more hope and renewed kidney function, I hid my fears behind a reluctant smile and shuffled back to the boat.

We twisted and turned, dodging floating logs and large driftwood bouncing up and over the wake of larger day river vessels, which were working the waters. We were now well underway, and had left Iquitos City behind us, once and for all. For the first couple of miles or so, families of Indians lined the riverbank waving goodbye, some wearing native coverings, others oddly wearing what looked like red Manchester United football shirts. But that would soon all disappear as we drew deeper into the jungle and further away from civilisation.

Every so often we would see the odd lone Indian on the shore just standing there motionless and silent, watching us pass. Then the occasional carved out canoe would come into view up ahead, but then disappeared just as fast as we navigated the bends and searched out the little creeks for crocodiles, anacondas or Indian hunters.

After a couple of hours, it all became a little emotional as the reality of this expedition set in.

We knew we were embarking on something special and life changing. I still felt like I didn't want to get involved with anyone too much, so I sat minding my own business mainly occupying myself by gliding my hand along the surface of the water, although still being conscious of what might be lurking underneath.

There was a good even balance of men and women aboard,

ranging in ages from early twenties up to maybe mid-fifties that had ventured in from as far north as Canada to as east as Indonesia and New Zealand. They all had got to know each other before flying into Peru via internet group chats established once they had been booked on the trip through Smoothhead and the Spanish girl shaman a few months previous. I was the only stranger aboard who had joined at the last minute the day before, not knowing a soul.

I eventually began to loosen up and make the effort to get involved with one or two of the crowd I would be about to spend the next fifteen days with. Many remarked about the bravery it took for a person to venture alone in pursuit of the medicine and this played to the beat of my conviction to keep going. Little did they know what darkness dwelled in me; the consequences of a life lived wrongly that now plagued my every hour.

For the duration of the trip I had been glancing forward between heads, still trying to work out who Stella may have been with. Smoothhead and the girl shaman had spoken a lot with her sitting up front. She was sitting next to another American guy who seemed a little loud, but I could tell by their body language they were not an item.

For the first time in my life, I felt adamant that I wasn't going to easily get caught up in another reckless relationship, but that still didn't stop me from looking, liking and wondering. There was, without doubt, a real sense of freedom that seemed to accompany the decision to not get involved. It took some discipline, admittedly, but I had never been in that kind of mindset before. It felt empowering that for once in my life, even though I still very much yearned for completion, I could in fact hold back from jumping straight into fleshly desires and inevitably drowning in the process.

Like everything in my life at that time it was new-found territory I was finding myself in, but I was in a strange sort of way embracing some of it. I wondered what it might have been like to have been a eunuch, centuries beforehand. In a way, a relief I thought.

I had a mature insight whenever it came to weighing-up a crowd. It came with the criminal territory I had prowled around in. If you read the signs wrong in that world, you could be gone for a very long time, or even indefinitely. So, when I began to study her frame from a few rows back with well-tuned accuracy, I knew she was putting on a brave face. Though, she may have had the will to push on, I could sense her vulnerability. She was just about holding on by a thread.

As the saying goes 'It takes one to know one'. There was no doubt in my mind that we were all vulnerable in some way or another or we would not have been in the middle of nowhere, expecting to find the very thing we hadn't been able to find inside or outside of ourselves within the grips and deceptions of modern society. But for reasons concealed from me at the time, I felt a strong compulsion to protect Stella, like a duty thrust upon me, almost.

Well, we made it to the camp four hours later without capsizing and being eaten by piranha fish or crocodiles and I was glad for it. I was now apprehensively looking forward to getting down to the business I had gone there to do. The boat nudged up against the makeshift pontoon and we were greeted by two Shipibo tribesmen ready and waiting to help with our rucksacks and a hand ashore.

I was eager to step off the boat and stand on the bank, and I even began to feel like some sweaty, tough, Amazonian explorer with my bandana tied over my head.

I jumped off onto the flimsy platform and lit up a cigarette, contemplating what would be my home for the next two weeks.

One of the tribesmen began speaking with Smoothhead alone and then the New Zealander turned to us and shared what the Indian had spoken.

'The man has said that it's important when we wash in the river we should always do so in large numbers and never to bathe at night, alone, because of the large anaconda snakes that are around here. Take note, my friends, this is important advice.' Well, there was some macho murmuring among the men and nervous giggling among the women as they grabbed their rucksacks before making their way towards the wooden huts that awaited us all.

But I held back, alone.

I had always kept my distance in life. I had learned to keep the world away from myself and if they had ever thought to give out degrees in such a pursuit, I would have earned mine ten times over.

I had learned to conceal the fear inside so well and for so long that my own mother who brought me into this world would not have known anything different. So, I wasn't about to cave in now.

But—without doubt I was still a little concerned about the struggle I might have with the day-to-day team playing in the camp. The last time I had shared a closed space for any amount of time with a large number of people would have been twenty years previous when I had been serving prison time. Somehow, I had managed to stay out of jail since that period but in short, my whole life had been one constant prison term. Every stinking hour of every stinking day, I found no peace or remission from my double mindedness. I was sure I'd been given two souls at birth and neither one would agree with the other.

Therefore, no woman could fill me. No amount of drugs had been able to persuade me. All the booze I'd guzzled down had failed to give me the answers. The violence never liberated me, and any amount of cash could never complete me. Never knowing who I was, who I'd been born to be, I paid my way out of life. When in doubt I parted with a few quid to shut them up, to push them away from me.

So, to hold back the cloud of depression that constantly loomed, I wandered the earth in a booze fuelled, drug induced, fantasy world, hoping I would stumble across along the way, a truth that would set me free from all of the anguish and hopelessness that consumed my days, but it never came along.

However, there was still a vague expectation of the evil being wrenched out and a glimmer of hope that I might find my true identity there, in the jungle. The one that had somehow eluded me for so long. I was hoping for some kind of epiphany to take place, a wisdom and a peace given to me that would surpass all human understanding, but then, of course, the opposite could happen. I might go completely crazy and stay there in the wilds away from all civilisation and live out my days as a savage, hovering between this life and another.

I stood alone once more, with my rucksack over my shoulder but this time I was in the jungle considering a little bridge before me, held together with vines, further observing our small boat throw off its line, to then ease out of the creek into the fast flow of the River Amazon.

It was all a world away from anything or anyone I knew, and that vessel would not be returning until I had served my fifteen days in spiritual exploration. There was no way back, I was there for the duration, no matter what.

CHAPTER FOUR

A FREE LOVE THING

The women slept in a large timber hut that had been divided into half a dozen small bedrooms and the men were all together in another shed on the opposite side of the camp.

There were a few other, smaller shacks dotted around the camp with chickens running loose and fast between them and all the dwellings were elevated in common on stilts to be clear of the ground during the rainy season and the floods.

I looked over to the women's quarters but there was no sign of the girl with the darkened soul.

As I entered the men's dormitory it opened out into a large community area where I found the loud guy that had been sitting next to Stella now swinging with good momentum inside one of the handful of hammocks that hung all around in no set order. To my left was a long solid, crudely carved table, with two equally long benches, one either side.

Here is where we would meet each lunch and evening to eat and talk about how we were doing, although everyone except me had been following the ayahuasca diet up to two weeks before arriving, which meant they had been refraining from as much sugar and salt as possible.

This detox process was believed to help promote the healing benefits of the potion, so our diet for the two weeks would strictly be boiled eggs from the resident chickens, piranha fish caught early each morning around 3am from the river accompanied by brown rice and sweet bananas, watermelon or mangos harvested fresh from a nearby plantation.

I looked to the right and saw the doors to small rooms with large gaps at the top and bottom giving just enough privacy from the communal area. There were three either side of a little hall that at the far end led to another outside door. It slept all 6 guys including me. Smoothhead stayed in his own hut over the far end of the camp with the Spanish girl shaman.

As I was surveying the place, the guy in the hammock piped up. 'Yeah, that's it, you got it, straight through that little hall. I think yours must be the middle room on the left. Anyway, it's the only one left open, number six I believe. Hey, you should grab one of these when you're done!'

I stopped mid step and looked back at the man swinging gracefully.

'Say that again, the number I mean'

'I believe yours is number six', he repeated, just as he took a deep long draw on his mapacho cigarette before then exhaling a big blue cloud that bellowed out of the hammock into the hut.

I walked to the room, the only one left available, dropped my rucksack and stepped back from the beaten-up door that hung crooked on two old black leather straps. I had to focus hard at the painted number that had probably faded over time. Even in the dim light that the shack provided, I could see it was a clear 6.

I guess I had lived my life very superstitiously, coming from a background of spiritualism in my family. So, looking at this number in the fragile state I was in at that time, it wouldn't have taken much stretch of the imagination for me to have suspected there was something supernatural going on and room 6 was meant for me. It was same door number of the family home I had grown up in and now, in just a few days, it would be my forty third birthday. So, with so much talk of rebirth that had surrounded the whole river trip to the camp, I stood and wondered if I was about to be reborn in some way.

Right from the outset, Smoothhead had requested that we should refrain from smoking as it helped with the detox. However, I personally had no intention of giving up for the two weeks. There would be little else to do through the day other than swim and sit around counselling each other, which I was feeling a little apprehensive about.

But we all agreed to swim in numbers each day for safety and so before lunch most of us would walk a few hundred yards through the trees out into an opening near a bend on the river where the flow was much stronger. Not everyone was brave enough to do it, but most had a go.

We would stride into the creek which opened up much wider as we went further out. Then we would meet the current to grab and catapult us around the bend out into the straights, where we would then continue to glide on the surface for about a quarter of a mile, being taken by the strong force downstream. But we had to be mindful to swim at the right time in towards the bank, ready to then break free of the current and swim hard towards an opening where the Indians kept their canoes, and a flimsy pontoon washed from side to side.

It was easy to miss and then panic, desperately trying to grab onto a slippery tree root to prevent getting further pulled downstream.

I suppose we were all frightened of what lurked beneath the surface but found the nerve to somehow brave it each day anyway. The jungle humidity was so much that the river was the only respite we had from it. Mostly out of desperation we took the plunge; plus it was the only way of washing our bodies clean as we were all constantly drenched in sweat. The only cool time seemed to be between around 3am to 7am when the Indians left to fish. After that we were back in the oven.

I naturally began sharing my mapacho, so it didn't take long for my stash to run out. I think nearly all of the guys smoked, it became a good reason to gather together at the back door of our dormitory and get more familiar with each other.

Out of respect for Smoothhead, nobody wanted to own up that they were still puffing away, until he arrived at the back of the hut one day and asked me for a cigarette in front of them all which at that point eased the tension. When we got down to the last few though, we were sharing the same cigarette passing it around. We soon realised one of us was going to have to go trade with the Indians for some of their tobacco so I happily said I would go.

I had some Peruvian Sol, the local currency, left in my bag and one of the Indians, a guy about my age, was more than happy to sell me a bundle of around a hundred rolled mapacho. I asked how much he wanted for them waving the money in front of him, but he looked back at me and just shrugged his shoulders as he shoved them in my hand. So, I handed him a wedge of Peruvian currency. At that point his face broke out into a big goofy smile which said he was more than happy I supposed, and we shook hands.

Stella and me seemed to hit it off from the start. She smoked also, so that became our reason to sneak down to the river together. Standing on the bank smoking and dipping into the creek every sunset became a nice treat each day. But I was still not wanting to get too close and she was being respectful of that, although I had gotten the sense it wouldn't have taken much for the situation to have rapidly got out of hand. It became obvious pretty soon that there was an attraction between us, and for me, it felt like we had known each other for a long time. But it was still very important for me that I stayed neutral just like one of those eunuchs, at least until I knew I'd been fully healed.

I think secretly most of the group were weighing up who they fancied. Maybe it's just natural that people think that way, although there were no obvious signs of any two people pairing up at any point that I could see. There was one afternoon when I had walked out of my room to find Stella and Tom (the landing strip guy) swaying in sync, holding hands, side by side in two hammocks. I wasn't quite sure what to quite make of it. I guessed something might have happened between them, while I had been absent down on the riverbank or maybe I had just simply not seen the signs.

Although I had not shown her that kind of interest, it still felt a little unsettling seeing her change direction so keenly once she knew I wasn't there to get laid. Although, in a way it suited me. All I wanted really was to get well and get out of there, and chances are I was never going to see any of those people ever again.

I did wonder if it was a free love thing that she was trying to establish in the camp which no way would have floated my boat, but I couldn't have spoken of course for the others.

I had had my fair share of women in the past, but sharing I never liked. I left that to others.

I ventured down to the river on my own that night and even swam too, chancing my luck in the cool silky water.

I left it until the morning of my birthday before I said anything. I never was one to make a big deal anyway, but I thought I should say something. I only told Stella, expecting her to maybe keep it a secret, but she didn't. When it got to about five in the evening everyone began to gather, including the natives to sing Happy Birthday. A light spread of mainly fruit was laid out on the table, made up of watermelon, mango, bananas and plain popcorn. I never did get around to asking where the popcorn came from.

We had a little dance and I said a thank you speech which I was nervous about. I had only ever been best man at a wedding once, which was for my best pal 20 years before, and I had to get drunk to do it. But there would be no such luck in the jungle. Even so, I managed to get through it, I even got a little emotional, because I felt fully accepted into the group.

It was starting to become clear there was something in the anaconda snake that these tribal people seemed to revere, the very serpent spirit of the anaconda itself. I had never thought of an animal having a spirit, but these people without doubt seemed to not only believe it but knew it to be a very real thing. It went through all places high and low, taking the human spirit with it when under the influence of the ayahuasca potion. And on that journey, it was said, is where the healing would take place. All I knew was that just a few nights before I'd been holding the head of a large snake in my hands during the Gringo ceremony and it was as real as if holding my own skull. I even felt the texture of its skin and its eye openings.

As the sun began to go down, I wandered into the large ceremonial hut. There were handmade tapestries hanging on nearly every part of the circular wall. I had noticed that the older Shipibo woman would sit and hand sew them outside around the camp during the day and we were encouraged by Smoothhead to buy at least one of them each, out of courtesy, if nothing else.

I would go on to pick one, pointing it out to the old wrinkled lady that looked around a hundred years old, the soles of her feet like thick cow leather. She sat constantly chanting, rocking gently back and forth as she sewed each day.

The rest of the group were beginning to come in and lay down their yoga mats or sleeping bags in their individual places around the edge of the hut in preparation for the first midnight ceremony that awaited us. The young American who had had an interest in my tattoo was now sitting clothed in his white apparel, legs crossed, on his mat with his hands clasped around a clear glass skull that he had brought with him. His eyes were closed in search of something.

I circled the hut intrigued at every story inside their works of art. But it all seemed to point to one thing, the respect they had for the serpent spirit and its power. I stepped back outside and just stood watching the witchdoctor continue to stir the hot cauldron that hung securely over the heat of the fire. It was filled with river water and inside boiled the potion made up of the ayahuasca vine and the chacruna plant which we all had earlier helped to cut up and prepare, placing it into the pot.

The chacruna brings the hallucinogenic (DMT) effects which when activated in unison with the ayahuasca vine together bring the mix of consciousness and different aspects of awareness (the trip).

The Indian chanted as he stirred the pot which would go on for hours until reduced. Then at midnight we would all drink from its cup, coming totally under the authority of the witchdoctor and the effects of the spells he had placed into it, and also over us.

CHAPTER FIVE

THE CEREMONY

All fifteen of us were sat cross-legged, barefoot on our mats around the outer edge of the softly lit hut. We were roughly three metres apart, each of us wearing our white apparel.

Once I had agreed with Smoothhead to join the party back in Iquitos, I was asked to go and buy a loosely fitting white outfit so as to stay in keeping with the way they performed the rituals. I had also bought a polished ayahuasca stone from a street trader that I'd hung around my neck on black lace. It was an element of the whole ayahuasca journey that we should wear a piece of the root on our bodies as protection from negative spirits, so everyone in the camp wore at least one stone. Some were wearing two or three.

The dim light was coming from a handful of candles that had been carefully placed in a circle in the centre of the hut. Around the inner circle people were placing things like crystals and also handwritten notes addressed to people past and present in the hope of some kind of spiritual healing or reconciliation to take place.

On entry to the hut the Mediterranean girl shaman had slowly wafted burning Palo Santo all around our bodies in figure of eight shapes, one person at a time as we passed through. Palo Santo is a native wood that when burned gave off a strong sweet scent which the natives believed helped to repel evil spirits and negative energy. The shamans had been into both the men's and women's dormitories earlier in the evening fanning this scented smoke all around our rooms as well as blowing mapacho smoke over the door frames, for our spiritual protection in preparation for the night ahead.

Stella was positioned across from me on the opposite side of the circular hut where I could only just make out her silhouette in the low light. I wanted to go over and make sure she was doing OK before it all began. I quickly stood, and on tiptoes then crossed the timber boards as if out of politeness, not wanting to break the silence. I knelt down in front of her. It was dead quiet, other than the hum of the jungle which was always there. My knee cracked as I crouched down on her yoga mat and I knew that everyone in the room had heard, it was that hushed.

'How you doing?' I whispered, gently placing a hand on her shoulder.

She seemed a little distant, peering back at me through the darkness—'Yeah, I'm fine... really, I'm doing OK, Tony,' she uttered quietly, her head tilted back, resting against the timber.

'Whatever happens, just call out. I will try and find you, I promise' I whispered.

She smiled and said 'thankyou' tenderly under her breath. She knew what I meant.

It was deep, very deep and I didn't even know if it was possible. But I just wanted to reassure her she wasn't alone, that was all.

I stood up releasing my grip from her shoulder then headed back to my mat, the odd cough from a nervous seeker accompanying me across the darkened room. The candles helped also as they joined a tiny ray of moonlight entering in through the gap in the flimsy door.

I still knew where everyone was pretty much placed, but that wouldn't be for much longer. We were all about to journey out of our physical bodies, and away from where we lay in that wooden shack, some place in the southern hemisphere of planet earth. But where our souls would individually end up, no-one could know that, not one of us.

The witchdoctor entered the hut, carrying the vessel with the potion inside. With him was the shaman I'd bought the tobacco from. Both were dressed in white, but the witchdoctor wore a robe that hung down almost to the floor. The little old lady with the leather feet appeared also, ordained in her ceremonial white dress.

They stood together in a tight circle. The Mediterranean girl shaman, Smoothhead and the Indians each took their cup of potion then they broke away, making their way separately around the edge of the hut asking us each if we wanted a full or half cup. I chose half again, hoping this Shipibo brew would not be as strong as the Gringo's. Then I would go for a second cup a couple of hours in. That was the plan, anyway.

I took the potion along with everyone else then leant my back against the timber, closed my eyes and waited the 20 minutes for it to begin to work. The hut fell into a deep silence, only broken at first by the odd nervous cough.

But then the purging came. An orchestra of ridding sounds began to fill the darkness; then a long flushing out turned into a deep roar that resembled the grumble that had come from deep within me just four nights before, as Nicky had rolled around crying, in search of her loved ones.

I started to open and close my eyes to measure any differences in reality. The colours began to emerge, kaleidoscope shapes that went further away one behind another out into the distance. I pulled back, realising I had just lost some time. I had to open my eyes and look around. 'How long had that just been?' I wondered. I needed to check I was still sitting in the same place. I looked down at the cracks in the floorboards and realised I was.

I opened my eyes and the witchdoctor was sitting cross legged in front, just two feet away from me. He grinned, then the old lady came out from behind him and put the mapacho to his lips. He drew deeply on it, then she withdrew it as he blew the cloud all over me. His hand reached through the smoke and rested on the top of my stomach. Something began to wriggle around inside.

He began to chant in his native tongue an Icaros and then I started to heave, trying to vomit out the evil. Again, the same roar came up and out of me that had shook the hut during the Gringo ceremony. I sensed everyone go quiet at that point, even the jungle again. Every living creature was listening to this thing inside of me, protesting once more. The witchdoctor continued to chant over me and then the other natives began to gather around, wafting Palo Santo all around me. Why was I so special? I thought. I could hear others wailing and vomiting. But they just continued to stay close to me.

I then heard something coming out of Tom to my left. The shamans turned their attention to him just a few feet away. A loud wailing noise started coming from the landing strip guy. It sounded like some kind of Jurassic creature screeching and clicking. Tom was sat upright cross legged leant against the timber, his hands outstretched on each knee with his head down. I opened and closed my eyes many times attempting to refocus on what I was seeing, but the thing just looked the same every time I fixed my eyes upon Tom.

It looked thousands and thousands of years old. Its face made up of wrinkly skin, it had a large bald round head and its eyes were closed tight behind long slits either side of a flat wide nose. I watched it recede back down into Tom. As he simultaneously slowly lifted his head up level, his eyes then would open. Then Tom, the man, began shrieking and hollering just like the demon had done just a few seconds earlier. They were one and both the same thing.

Then Tom's eyes closed again, and he suddenly dropped his head in silence. The devil at that point rose up and out of Tom's body maybe three feet above his head, manifesting itself before us all in the room, nauseatingly wailing, squealing and clicking.

The shamans gathered in close to him, chanting, wafting Palo Santo but the thing continued to relentlessly protest, haunting us with every cry from hell.

Women were screaming, grown men were crying in fear of losing their souls, some even wanting to flee into the jungle. The natives encouraging them to stay on their knees faced away from the threat. The witchdoctor could simply not contain the evil that had gathered there in the hut that night and I began to vomit into a wooden bowl that had been handed me, but now just feet away the demon in Tom was seeking to align itself with the darkness in me and it began to stretch itself out my way.

It went in through my mouth and down into my gut and then I felt it inside my stomach. I tried to yell it away, 'Get out!', pushing my fingers down my throat to make myself vomit and then eventually the spirit receded pulling back to Tom, clicking and wailing as it went. The girl shaman sat in front of me and began chanting an Icaros trying to protect me from the onslaught. But she had no control over the devil's will. Again, it came into me through my mouth joining up with the darkness inside. 'Get out of me!' I tried to yell it away again, but my energy was gone, nothing came out. I just continued to retch and heave attempting to vomit it free, pushing my fingers down my throat.

I tried to escape its grip by standing up and getting away from Tom, but I got to my knees and could not find the strength to clamber to my feet. I fell down and rolled over on my side away from it. I lay there holding my throat tight, almost strangling myself to try and prevent it from coming in anymore, but it still found a way as I attempted in vain to protect myself.

'I'm not evil, you're not coming into me!' I gurgled, out into the room in a pathetic show of defiance, but it was too late for all that. Who was I to tell the devil he had no rights over me? I wrestled with that demon all night. It was the hardest fight of my life.

I had tried to look for Stella at some point in all of the confusion but couldn't find her. By all accounts, she had just sat silently all the way through it.

As the sun came up and the potion wore off, we all could not believe what we had experienced that night. Shuffling around at dawn with spun out eyes and mouths wide open, 'what was that thing?' had been the common question we all had asked each other.

All I wanted to do was get out of the camp and find a way back to Iquitos.

The shamans were simply way out of their depth and they hadn't the power to deal with the demon that had manifested itself.

Everyone kept a wide berth from Tom around the camp from then on, including Stella.

I spoke to Tom wanting to know where he thought the demon had come from. He then admitted that he had gone to the jungle in the hope he might get set free from it. He said that he felt something enter him one night when he was meditating using crystals with a sorcerer he had invited into his home.

Repeatedly I tried to talk to Smoothhead, telling him that he and the natives should take Tom out to the tree in the jungle, the one which they called the sacred tree. Tie him to it and expel the spirit well clear of the people in the camp. But he returned with the comment that it had been a collective of evil in the hut and that it wasn't all inside Tom.

I guess at that point he made sense. How could I have personally argued with that possibility? But over the next two days running up to the second ceremony I still tried to convince the rest of the group to not go back in for more, telling them they didn't have to feel forced to do so. But they see it wiser to keep to the program and stay close to Smoothhead and the Indians.

In the end I decided to stay on, as there was no obvious way back to Iquitos. I had no army experience and so I didn't fancy the idea of trekking through the jungle without a compass with no way of knowing which way I was heading. Maybe I could have followed the river back to Iquitos, but then there was the possibility of succumbing to a wild animal. The natives did have small canoes which they fished with, but Smoothhead knew that if I left this way, some of the others, if not all of them, would want to leave also. So, he persuaded me to stay on and I reluctantly agreed.

CHAPTER SIX

HELP US!

Two days later, they all began to prepare for the next ceremony. As the time neared midnight, I feared what was about to happen. Everyone gathered once again in the community part of the men's dormitory, wearing their white apparel. One or two looked reasonably relaxed swinging in the hammocks, but the majority of the group that sat on the table and benches looked nervous and there was a fear hanging in the air. The shamans had carried out the same ritual as before, cleansing the dormitories and all of the living spaces with Palo Santo and mapacho.

I tried to quietly persuade some of them, including Stella, to not go back in, but they refused to listen and felt somehow safer in the hands of the shamans even though the natives had done nothing to try and help Tom since. Whatever that thing was, it most definitely would still be in him and so I would take my chances and hang well back alone. One by one the seekers walked out from the community area and headed across the camp towards the ceremony hut, under candlelight, to meet the girl shaman who awaited them.

She stood just outside the door, burning Palo Santo again, wafting it all around their bodies in figure of eight shapes in a futile attempt to repel the evil spirits before they entered the ceremony hut.

Their smoking dead wood had done very little two nights before, and I had no confidence their burning scent would be any match a second time for that demon and its influence over the camp.

The last seeker finally entered, then Smoothhead closed the door behind her. I sat on the steps of the men's quarters just listening to the jungle, looking all around the perimeter of the camp as far as my eyes could see, and my spine shuddered at the thought of what darkness was about to be awoken.

I heard a rustling coming from a thicket of trees and I strained in the pitch black to see where it was coming from. But then as I my eyes began to adjust a little better, I saw it was the tribesman I had got the tobacco from. He made his way straight towards me. He was smoking a mapacho and passed it, telling me to put it to my mouth and smoke. He then waved his hand for me to back up into the hut and stay inside. I could tell by his face he was fearful also. He looked concerned for my wellbeing, telling me it would be much safer inside.

I did as I was warned, then once I was inside, he lit another mapacho and began blowing it around the door frame of the hut, which he honestly believed would help protect me. He then left and I saw him no more that night.

It wasn't long before the purging began again among the seekers in the ceremony hut, followed by violent vomiting which lasted some time, but then abruptly the camp fell silent, dead silent.

Again, it seemed even the jungle mutterings came to a stop as though every creature was now paying homage to the witchdoctor's spiritual advances. Over ten minutes must have passed before the shaman broke the silence with a song.

Then it started...

I began to feel sick and dizzy, so I grabbed my sleeping bag and slipped into the hammock furthest from the entrance door. I didn't want to be in my room. I thought my best option was to stay in the open community area of the dormitory so I would have a good view of the door opening. I covered myself over, laid back into the hammock and tried to stay calm.

I couldn't help thinking that my life must be cursed. But then I thought of my four beautiful daughters back in England that I loved, trying to reassure myself that I had indeed been afforded some goodness in my life and it wasn't all completely bad. The warm picture of my girls helped momentarily to block out the tremendous fear. But I couldn't help but hold my head in my hands detesting the man I had become as my stomach continued to turn over.

I rolled out of the hammock onto the floor and stayed there on all fours, then I heard the human groaning cease. Again, a deafening silence fell over the camp. I looked up at the open doorway scared something might enter. I stayed low down and kept still, waiting for something to change in the ceremony hut. But then my worst fear become the reality I'd been dreading.

The long silence was eventually broken and the thing inside Tom started wailing, groaning and clicking once more and the seekers began to cry out in fear of their lives for the second time.

I grabbed my blanket from the hammock and moved to the end of the table away from the entrance that had no door, and even though it was humid I wrapped the blanket around my shoulders trying to feel a little more protected. There were hours left to go before dawn.

Having nowhere to turn, I put my head into my hands and tried to hide from the hell I was in, locking my eyes shut. In my mind I flashed back to those early innocent years before all the evil had crept into my life and remembered that bright sunny morning, when my mum had slipped her hand from mine, blowing me a sweet kiss as I entered the church. I looked back for her, but she was gone. Then the man slammed the heavy wooden doors. The blinding shards of light came through the colourful stained-glass windows and I had to put my hand up to shield my eyes so I could see the figure on the cross.

'HELP ME, JESUS!' I audibly cried out into the hut, tears pouring from my eyes. But I kept them locked tight, continuing to watch that little boy stood looking up at the man on the cross. I cried out again, 'Jesus, I'm scared, I'm so afraid, please, protect those frightened people out there. Jesus, HELP US!!' I continued to pray in desperation, too afraid to lift up my head.

I was still sat at the far end of the community table eating some fruit when one of the shamans came in to the mens dormitory and sat across from me, early that same morning. 'Was you praying last night?' he asked me. I looked at him. 'How could he have known that?' I thought to myself. 'He never left the ceremony hut, not once all through the night'. 'I was praying, yes,' I said.

He studied my eyes. 'Who was you praying to?' he replied, briefly looking away to peel a banana but then his eyes swiftly reconnected, as he tried to telepathically read my thoughts. 'Jesus,' I simply replied. 'I was praying to Jesus'. He stood up stone faced, void of all expression and without saying anything further he left the table.

They continued with their ceremonies every other night, but some of the seekers began to pull away also, refusing to take part, choosing to stay in the community hut with me. Those few that held back then chose to burn lots of Palo Santo and blew mapacho all around the doorframe of our hut, in the hope of some protection during the long nights.

But I kept my head down sat alone at the end of the table, praying to the man on the cross each evening until it was finally over.

At last the fifteen days came to an end and the boat returned from Iquitos to take us out of there.

I was glad to see that boat moor up in that creek, and I was glad to be heading back to the natural world and hopefully some sanity. But there was no way I was going to be able to judge how the whole thing had affected me until I hit civilisation again and focused on some kind of normality.

I fully understood then why those seekers all looked so battle worn when getting off the boats, wandering away with that aimless empty look on their faces, while I sat drunk, observing them from the safety of the bar just two weeks prior. I now felt the same defiled numbness inside that they had projected. We got back to the town without saying much all along the river journey and headed straight to La Casona. It was not spoken about, the evil we had all witnessed in the jungle. It quickly became shelved under a taboo.

Most had their rooms pre-booked to stay on in the town a further day or two, but some were leaving that same day on scheduled flights out to Lima. Tom was one of them leaving and no sooner had we got back to the hotel he was making arrangements for a motorcycle-taxi to take him to Iquitos airport. He offered to return my shorts and T-shirt that I had lent him, but I told him he could keep them. I didn't even want to wear anything he had been wearing in case it was possible for something evil to be transferred, I was feeling that cautious.

I found it difficult to embrace the guy as he stood up in the courtyard of the La Casona, where we were all gathered to say our goodbyes. But I brought myself to shake his hand, telling him to make it a priority to seek help when he got back to England and to get that thing expelled. But in my mind, I wondered if there really was realistically any help out there, for him or for me. Surely, he needed to undergo some kind of exorcism I thought as I loosened my grip. He thanked me for my concern and said he would try his best to get help.

It turned out Stella was booked on the same flight out of Iquitos with Tom. They would also transfer at Lima together and fly into Dallas where they would then separate and go their different ways, Stella onto Oregon and Tom back to the UK, so they were saying their goodbyes together. I still wondered if they were going to get it on, although I couldn't really imagine her wanting to chance it.

I was concerned for Stella in that way. To me it was obvious that during the whole trip she had been reaching out for male attention and it became apparent that, although she wasn't wearing any wedding ring, she was in fact married. She had cried a lot in the camp over her marriage and she seemed to have reached out to the group many times, both to the men and women during the two weeks in the jungle saying how her intimate relationship with her husband was finished and that they had been sleeping in separate rooms for years. She expressed how they were more like brother and sister than lovers.

It was time for her to walk to me for a hug. It had been a trip not one of us would forget and I was sad to see her leave so fast. I had been hoping to take a little walk around town together, just the two of us and maybe have some dinner. But she was booked on the flight and had to leave.

She gave me a hug, then pulled out her cell phone asking me for my number and email address. I gave it to her, then she wrote her details down on a piece of paper and handed it to me.

I carried her luggage out to the awaiting motorcycle-taxi and hugged her one last time before she hopped aboard next to Tom. As they pulled away, she looked behind waving until they turned a corner, out of sight. I stood there in the road, feeling sunken and alone once again with a new question looming. What do I do now?

It was said that the effects of the potion could last up to six months and so all I could do was keep going and hope for the best. I had lost a lot of body fluid and fat whilst in the jungle, so at least there had been some benefit that was obvious to the eye. I wondered if I had been cured of the booze. Of course, it all depended on whether the depression was gone, because the two had always lived side by side, feeding each other's needs. The date on my return flight to London was not for another four weeks, although I had no intention of leaving Peru until I felt sure I was cured. I needed time to find out if there had been any benefit at all from taking the potion.

The rest of the group were making arrangements to fly into the Sacred Valley in the Andes mountains, visiting Machu Picchu the Inca citadel ruins high up in the clouds. This is where they would gather together on the mountain and participate in a similar kind of ceremony.

They were planning to drink San Pedro, another ancient potion which induces a psychedelic experience. At that point it seemed to be more about the buzz than a genuine search for true healing and restoration and I had no interest in going any further with them.

I wished them well in their extended search for the truth, as I said my farewells and packed my things. I left La Casona a day earlier than they planned to, with the sole intention of getting a head start on them, flying into Lima, to then catch a flight into the Sacred Valley where I could find some open space and get lost for a while, alone in the mountains.

CHAPTER SEVEN

THAT UNEQUIVOCAL SOMETHING

Once I arrived in Cusco, I decided to book myself into the Marriot hotel for a couple of nights as a luxury treat. I enjoyed the good food and the spa facilities, especially breathing the coca leaf in during a steam room session. By seeking this comfort, I guess a little bit of snobbery may have been rising up, although of course, I had only ever been a thug. Nonetheless I had enjoyed the luxuries easy wealth had brought me in the past, lounging around in posh hotel spas with gangland associates, dreaming up new ways to gain more cash and stay ahead of the authorities. This of course was a made-up identity, although I realised many onlookers secretly aspired to the lifestyle.

Celebrating being away from all of the madness of the jungle, I hit the booze that night, sampling their local Cusquena beer and downing shots of their Pisco sour, the Peruvian equivalent to tequila in the hotel bar. I woke up in my room the next morning struggling to breathe because of the height of the town in the Andes mountains and the combination/ amount of alcohol and mapacho I had consumed. It all combined brought on altitude sickness. So, with the lack of breath and nausea I began to go into a cold and sweaty almost delirious panic.

The hotel sent a doctor to my room towing an oxygen bottle along with him. I laid there with the mask strapped to my face slowly regaining my breath as the doctor regularly checked my blood oxygen level. He then recommended I consume coca leaf tea to combat the sickness, so I made it a thing to sit and drink a large pot each morning, and it worked.

I watched a movie once about three men lost in the Alaskan wilderness. Their small propeller driven plane hit a flock of migrating birds which forced them to crash land into a freezing lake. For many days a man-eating Grizzly was on their trail, stalking them. He kills and eats one of the men, forcing the other two to take desperate action to try and survive. They would either have to defeat the man killer or most surely it would devour them. When they finally chose to face the evil and fight back, their courage paid off, they killed the bear and ended the threat on their lives.

After walking for days, lost without food, shivering in the harsh conditions, they now had fresh meat to eat and a large bear skin for body coverings. They had turned a corner, and now as the two men stood on a high ridge looking out over the rugged, harsh beauty of the wilderness before them, with food in their bellies and bear skin for warmth, what seemed impossible yesterday now looked not only doable, but hopeful, even inviting. The older of the two, a rich man that had had everything money could bring in his life, spoke up.

'You know, all my life, I always wanted to do something that was unequivocal, all of my life'. The second man turned to his companion and replied with a smile 'My friend, I think this might just qualify.'

All of my life, I too had always wanted to do something that would leave no doubt. Something unmistakable. I too wanted to stand on a ridge and look out at a complete change and embrace it with courage and full commitment, never looking back once in fear or doubt at the world I was leaving behind.

I left the very comfortable Marriot hotel and moved into a room on the other side of town. On the way, I wandered into the Gothic Cathedral of Cusco that towered over the Plaza de Armas.

I wasn't sure what I was looking for, the same security I guess I had experienced in the jungle when I had cried out in fear to the man on the cross. Maybe I just wanted to say thanks in some way, sit quietly in one of the pews and stay dry whilst the storm passed over.

Every day at some point a storm darkened, the skies pouring heavy rain down on the town, which would then bounce up off the cobbled streets almost three feet. Being high up in the Andes at nearly 3500 metres above sea level the weather seemed that much closer, and so when the lightening flashed, and the thunder came moments later, the rumble travelled through the Sacred Valley with a real eeriness. In a screwed-up kind of way I was enjoying this experience, because that storm happening outside somehow reflected what was going on in me.

Although I sat quietly, safe inside the church, away from it all, at least momentarily anyway, I found a peace in just thanking God for helping me through that recent hell. And so, I decided I would buy a crucifix on a chain to wear around my neck. I said thank you one last time before heading back out into the heavy rain to go and see one of the many silversmiths in the town that made and sold quality hand-made jewellery.

As I walked the back streets of Cusco, I began to purposely look for a reason to stay there in the mountains. 'Could my purpose in life be linked to this place?' I considered as I sat and drank my usual pot of coca leaf tea smoking mapacho on an outside table of one of the many cafés in the town. I thought of buying a large building I had seen for sale and converting it into a children's orphanage. I didn't know any statistics, if there was a real need there in the Sacred Valley, although I didn't need to look too hard to see the poverty all around me. I remembered that when I was in the company of kids, I became like one and I could revisit innocence.

I spoke to a woman working as an agent for the sellers of this very large Spanish house that conveniently sat a couple of blocks from the centre of town that I had visualised being the perfect premises. I even took a viewing, walking around this huge private home with its large cobbled inner courtyard and many spacious rooms that could be easily converted into sleeping dormitories, a classroom, kitchen, dining area, shower and toilet facilities, medical room, TV and games rooms.

The old colonial home with its secure gated grounds seemed ideal and I started to get excited about the possibility of this being my real vocation in life. Maybe I wasn't meant to go back to London and perhaps I was now looking at that unequivocal something I had been longing for all this time.

I took the agent's number and told the lady I would be in touch and that I was in the area for at least one month. But then, I thought, 'How could I really do something like this alone? Surely, I would need to meet a good woman who would help me run the place and look after the kids.'

In the jungle I had been reintroduced to the pendulum. I remembered as a child the adults in the family dangling a silver or gold necklace chain over the belly of any of the pregnant women of the family to see what sex the child would be born. We had moments in the jungle where we would take off our ayahuasca stones from around our necks and dangle them out in front, asking the spirits to answer questions by moving the pendulum. We would say to it, 'Make a circle if it's a no or swing in a straight line if it's a yes', then we would ask the question. I had no clue at the time that I was asking evil spirits for guidance.

I sat on the end of my bed in my hotel room in Cusco needing some quick answers, so I took off the silver crucifix and chain from around my neck and dangled it out front asking it to show me answers to the questions I was asking but it wouldn't move. Every time I asked the same questions, 'Is this orphanage idea for me? Will I meet the woman who will help me run it?' but the cross with Jesus on it would not move. It stayed hanging in the centre of my palm.

I then took off the ayahuasca stone from around my neck and asked the same question and immediately it swung in favour telling me I was on the right track. I then I asked the second question whether I would meet the woman who would help me. Again, it swung with strong momentum to one side but then stopped at a 45-degree angle in mid-air for at least 2 seconds before it swung back down very slowly and controlled and stopped dead still in the centre of my palm. This disturbed me as I hadn't seen this happen before in such a precise manner, so I didn't ask the spirits anything else from then on.

A week after leaving the jungle I was still seeing green kaleidoscope patterns whenever I closed my eyes and also the same evil faces which I had seen during the Gringo ceremony. The image of the demon that had manifested through Tom just wouldn't get out of my head. I realised I had seen far too much and could never go back to looking at life the same way ever again. The devil and his army of demons really did exist, but what could I do with this horrifying truth?

I wanted to just forget the whole thing, but I knew deep down I would never be able to. I started to wonder how the others were getting on. Were they kept awake in despair also?

Ignorance really is bliss, I thought. Some things are better left unknown. I had sought illegitimate divine wisdom and in return been given a truth I couldn't handle.

At night whenever trying to sleep, I would be looking at a pair of cold reptilian eyes staring back at me when closing mine, like they were a part of me, and I could not settle unless I was intoxicated with alcohol. I had to block out what I didn't understand, and I started to become fearful again that I really was doomed and there was no way out for me. Feeling more and more tremendously alone, all I could do was put one foot in front of the other and see where I ended up.

I decided to leave Cusco and head north to stay at the little sleepy ancient Inca town of Ollantaytambo. I arrived there after enjoying the long, occasionally bumpy, drive through the Sacred Valley. With the window down in the back of the beaten-up old taxi I observed the shepherds in the far distance wearing their colourful woven garments leading their alpaca herds over mountain passes and occasionally across the road directly in front of us. This, momentarily, put a smile on my face, taking my mind away. How free that shepherd's life had looked from where I was sitting and what I would have given right then to have swapped garments with him, disappearing into the mountains void of the afflictions that were now haunting my every move.

I watched the taxi pull away, leaving me in the square, feeling like I was standing in some dusty forgotten terracotta town. And this seemed to align with the whole lonely abstract state that was now my reality as I watched myself stood at an eternal junction that offered no sign home. Like in a dream, I was walking aimlessly across a suspicious wasteland and unless I found the missing piece of the jigsaw, I would never wake up and make it back. And the possibility that I had died in that trailer on that cliff top in Peacehaven just one month before started to seriously jar me also.

'Could it be I'd overdosed and was now dead, just existing in limbo, this place not being real at all?'

The thought made me feel sick with guilt and tremble with a crushing, shameful humiliation.

'Who found me dead then? Was I shamefully naked, surrounded with dozens of empty brandy and vodka bottles? Large holdalls of cash held up in the wardrobe. A handful of blackened, makeshift crack pipes in the sink. Small empty packets smeared with the bitter remnant of wet amphetamine, scattered randomly on the coffee table. The laptop still open, revealing my secret love affair with loneliness?' I heaved to be sick, but nothing came up.

As I wiped my mouth, I saw a sign for a room available which led me up a narrow, cobbled hill where at the top a small hotel stood detached. They had one room left so I paid and then took the key from the man at the desk, refusing the offer of a light snack. It was getting late and I just wanted to rest, but as I put the key in the lock, it wouldn't turn. I tried a few times before walking back downstairs to make sure I had the right one. He checked and it was the correct key.

Returning to the door it still would not open trying for what must have been five minutes before the man from Reception arrived to help. He then took the key from me, inserted it and turned the lock without any problem. I said, 'thankyou', a little embarrassed, then waited for him to leave before trying it myself both from the inside of the room and outside. This time both ways it opened with ease. I didn't like the way I was feeling, as if being monitored by some invisible intelligence. And now tricks were being played on me. I just needed a drink. Even more so now, the booze was being more of a friend to me than it ever had been before. I decided I needed to plug back into home reality which I hoped still existed and would give me some balance and orientation, so decided to check my emails as I hadn't done so since landing in Peru. I remembered seeing a little place in the square earlier that offered internet, so I made my way there.

As I headed back down the hill, a mountain storm began to move in over the town, darkening the place almost completely, bringing lightning, thunder and rain with it. Being mindful not to slip, I started to run through the narrow backstreets, past stable doors to small terracotta coloured homes. The upper part of the doors to some of the houses were still swung wide open regardless of the heavy storm, and so I waved as I went by, nodding with courtesy to the curious natives sat in their living rooms.

Inca children were peeking at me from behind walls, but then as I reached the corner they were gone as I continued to run through the heavy rain which now overflowed the drainage gullies either side of the maze of cobbled pathways. I eventually reached the shack in the square that posed as an internet café.

I was surprised to see that Stella had been in touch so soon. In fact, she had sent me two emails, the first one asking me if I was still in Peru and if so, what part? The second one was asking why I hadn't replied to the first email which she had sent just the day before the second one. It seemed as soon as she had arrived back into the US, with itchy feet, she had wanted to board another plane and leave again. She was clearly frustrated with her home life because she hadn't even unpacked her rucksack, she wrote.

As I read her message, I sensed there was a real possibility she might want to join me in the Andes, leaving behind her life there in the US, never to look back. Maybe she was the one the pendulum had swayed in favour of. I knew there had been more in it than just that platonic friendship we had shared in the Amazon.

I was desperate and couldn't wait to return an email inviting her back out and went on to tell her all about the orphanage idea and how it seemed like it could be destiny that she had chosen to get in touch so soon. I asked if it would be something she might like to be a part of and that I hoped that she would agree to join me. 'If she does, my haunted nights alone with the devil would be over' I thought. And, sure enough, she returned an answer almost straight away agreeing to come out as soon as she could saying she loved the orphanage idea. She booked a flight that same night to Lima and then on to Cusco where she would be landing in just two days time. I celebrated by getting paralytic drunk in the small empty bar in the square, before zig zagging my way back to my room and passing out.

The next day I headed back to Cusco in preparation for Stella landing, booking us into a hotel which when I looked out of the bedroom window, surprisingly had a clear view of Christo Blanco, the 8-metre-high white statue of Christ Jesus which stood on a hilltop guarding over the ancient city.

CHAPTER EIGHT

MOTH TO CANDLELIGHT

It was late, close to midnight as we both stood holding hands smoking from the window of our hotel room looking out over the city night lights of Cusco. The full moon had come around once more and was now so low and large in the sky that its beam fully illuminated the figure of Christo Blanco, standing with His arms outstretched in compassion, beckoning the nations to turn to Him, away from the witchcraft which had infiltrated the hearts of all men.

I couldn't help but notice though, it was the moon Stella was fixated on, and not the beauty of the statue of Christ. She seemed charmed I would say, even spellbound until she broke her gaze to take a long slow draw on her cigarette. But then her eyes soon readjusted back up to it as she lazily channelled the thick blue fog from her lungs out through the window where it was met and taken swiftly by the cool night air.

She then slowly turned her attention to me, clenching my hand tighter while a mild childish giggle erupted impromptu, as if she'd been somehow caught out by me watching her. I then noticed a darkening of her eyes, like the shadow of something passing by the window, but there was nothing there. She continued to stare up at me, still smiling and tightly gripping my hand, as then I observed her childlike mischievous expression regress to something sensual and darkly seductive which I sensed was old, maybe even ancient, in its wisdom. And it lured me like a moth to candlelight.

The fear in me had strangely subsided since becoming intimate with Stella. And so, I didn't feel the need to share all at once, the full extent of what had been happening since leaving the Amazon. We had not mentioned, either of us, what had gone on in the jungle. For me it was too soon to go back and relive. But I was at a last feeling some ease as Stella uncannily began mirroring those deep things inside, those lifelong aspirations that few knew about. 'Surely this is meant to be', I thought. 'She knows too much for it not to be'.

Kindred spirits, she said, we were twin souls that had been lost in time but had finally found their way back to each other. It couldn't have come at a better point. I desperately needed to know that someone who understood deep things had my back, somebody I could trust that would let me know if I was doing OK and therefore hadn't slipped away into complete madness. And it seemed Stella had turned up to do exactly just that.

We were drinking coffee one morning in the small ancient market town of Pisac just a few miles from the city of Cusco, watching the Inca people silently go about their early morning ritual of setting up their stalls and laying out their alpaca products and locally handmade silverware and leatherware in preparation for the handful of tourist coaches that came daily from the city. As we sat at our table outside the small hotel we were staying in, we warmed ourselves in the early morning sun. I then began to explain how for a long time I harboured a dream of owning a large country estate or farm and work with horses.

At that moment her face detonated into a youthful excitement. She then went on to tell me how she had spent most of her teenage school vacations working hard on her uncle's ranch, herding cattle and looking after the horses. She insisted, full of beans, that if the orphanage thing didn't exactly work out for some reason, she would want nothing more than to live out that kind of life and if I was really serious about it, Texas would be the best US state to find the perfect dream ranch. She then immediately began looking up real estate websites on her phone, signing up to a few of them to receive their weekly online brochures.

I had hit rock bottom and this life had very nearly destroyed me. But now I had met this attractive and very intuitive woman, who appeared to know me better than I did myself and better still she wanted the exact same things out of life as I did. It seemed a very real last chance was now revealing itself and I was feeling for the first time since leaving London right about the choice I had made in journeying to Peru.

I didn't really know where to begin but I was eager to get started and so I put a low offer in for the Spanish Colonial house close to Cusco's central square, just to see what reception I would receive from the closed off, shy locals by rattling their cage a little. Plus, I needed to focus on something. We were both boozing heavily each day. Stella could easily match my drinking, so we needed a direction. They were asking $1,200,000 for the freehold, so offered them $900,000.

I also wanted to show Stella that I was serious about the plans I had for the orphanage and I wasn't a guy that talks and doesn't do. But mainly I was desperate to make changes and move towards my dream of escaping my past and starting over again.

I knew that with the sale of a property I owned in London plus digging up the holdall of cash I had vacuum sealed and buried in the ground I would easily cover the figure I had offered the vendor plus have a few quid left over to set the orphanage up and get it rolling.

On the other hand, she thought I was crazy, running ahead without checking first on what the local legal requirements were and also the small detail of how it would be continually funded. Mouths need feeding every day. Instead, she suggested we should do our homework first and maybe visit one or two orphanages to get a better understanding of how it all worked. After all, neither of us had a clue how to run a children's home.

It made perfect sense, so we began asking around and after speaking to one or two locals a registered tour guide put us in touch with a social worker. She agreed over the phone to meet with us one morning in our hotel reception for a chat and a coffee.

She was a smartly dressed, straight talking woman that offered her credentials up on first arriving. I could see she was all above board, she wasn't a con artist that had met with us for personal gain. She was clearly dedicated to the welfare of the kids she'd been entrusted to oversee, and she also spoke good English which helped the meeting along. She went on to explain how she worked closely with a small children's home situated on the outskirts of Cusco, the population of around 30 or so kids being made up of young girls ranging in age from 6 to 17.

I asked when we could go there. She made a call and arranged for us to drive out there the following morning. I asked how we could donate some money to the place. 'Should we take cash?'. She insisted that we should, on no account, give the guy that ran the home money, because he was a gambler and would only put it in his back pocket, the kids wouldn't see a penny. This made me want to string the guy up before I'd even laid eyes on him. Instead, she suggested to buy food for the kitchen as the annual Mothers-day celebration fell on the upcoming Sunday and they would all appreciate a good hearty meal together. This thought put a smile on my face and sounded like a good plan.

She picked us up early the next morning and drove us to the local market where we purchased choice meats and vegetables for them to cook their Sunday meal. We all had our hands full as we carried the heavy bags through the bustling market crowd out to the car, but then I asked about dessert. 'All kids love ice cream; shouldn't we get them some?' I said. The social worker said they were not used to such treats, but we all agreed they should have a nice bowl of ice cream each after their meal. So, we stopped at a couple of stores clearing their freezers out till we calculated we had enough to go around.

CHAPTER NINE

MARIA

Outside the orphanage, every ground floor window had steel mesh on the outside like a prison and the front entrance was through a large pair of wooden garage doors that had a steel security gate in front. Young thugs started to gather in the street like they controlled the place, they were curious about the Gringos now arriving at the girls' home. How come they didn't know we were arriving?

The social worker then turned on a hand-held walkie talkie and said something in Spanish to someone inside. One of the garage doors opened a few minutes later and a teenage girl about 17 with a big glowing smile dressed in a dirty pink tracksuit opened the security gate keeping inside, holding the other radio. She then said something which came through into the car. After looking up the street both ways she beckoned us to quickly head inside. At that point the social worker told us to get out and start grabbing the food bags from the car.

When the lady had said the place was located on the outskirts of the town, for some reason I envisaged somewhere a bit more rural and serene, but this place was the ghetto and obviously a danger spot. Therefore, sure enough, as I opened the boot to start taking the food out a teenage kid rode past very closely on a pushbike nodding at me with his mind on something ugly, his expression clearly not being a friendly one, rather a dark, blank, hungry look of menace was written all over his face. He scanned the situation to relay to his gang up ahead. But I winked back at the kid with the same face he had given me, warning him I spoke their language and whatever was in their heads, they should think again. I then opened the rear car door and helped Stella out before we all began hastily getting the bags from the car into the building.

There inside was the whole residence of 30 or so kids all different ages standing in a long line passing the food bags along until they reached the kitchen out the back with big infectious smiles of appreciation spread all across their faces. I couldn't help but notice how dirty their mainly pink clothes were, heavily stained, clearly not having been washed for some time, but the girls' faces themselves looked washed and amazingly happy as we began shaking each of their hands once all the food was inside and the security gate had been locked tight.

The bare brick walls were damp from roof leaks and puddles of rainwater gathered in corners of the cold concrete floor and the place stank of mildew. As we passed the downstairs kitchen it screamed of bad hygiene and as I looked inside it appeared rotten dirty, and I couldn't put my finger on the sickening stench either.

We were then led up a steel fire escape to the first-floor landing, which was partly open to the outside elements before entering into the large reception room that was also used as the dining area, with a long table and chairs in one part and lots of sofas joined together on the other side with a small pile of board games neatly stacked on a large communal coffee table.

Gina, the girl security guard, seemed to be also in charge of the kids. After she spoke privately with the social worker, Gina informed us that the director had urgent business to attend in Lima and had to leave early that same morning, so she would show us around instead. This teenage kid was level-headed and polite and clearly showed mothering instincts, looking out for the rest of the younger bunch. I warmed to her straight away, admiring her strength. I had daughters back home and I couldn't help but feel immediately protective of her and the poverty these kids were living in was already starting to pull terribly on my heartstrings. I wanted to do something for them. She offered to make us coffee, but we politely declined for fear of what germs might have lurked in the kitchen. She began showing Stella and me around the girls' bedrooms whilst the social worker stayed behind to catch up with the others.

All the time we could hear this sobbing coming from one of the rooms at the end of the landing on the second floor above where we were walking. I asked Gina why the girl was crying. She said in good enough English for us to understand that the girl had only just arrived that morning having been taken from her abusive home, her father being a violent alcoholic, but she hadn't stopped weeping since she arrived. I asked her name. 'Maria', she said. We went into every room except Maria's.

Broken, cracked windows that were left for the cold mountain wind to enter were found in nearly every bedroom. The sheets and blankets were damp and rotten dirty. After seeing a few rooms, I'd had enough and asked Gina if they were all the same. She nodded her head with a smile as if nothing was wrong, as if I was asking a strange question. I had to assume the girl just hadn't known things to be any better.

I turned, leaving Stella to continue the tour with Gina and walked back to Maria's door peeking through the gap. She was sat on the end of her bed faced away from the door towards her broken window where two pigeons fluttered around noisily, fighting for the use of the outside ledge. All the time she continued to weep with her head down in cupped hands. I swallowed hard and pushed on along the landing. We cut the tour short and headed back down to the reception area where everyone was now gathered for a talk.

We sat for a while and spoke to all the girls, although most didn't speak English, but Gina and the social worker easily translated for us. The kids mostly spoke with big smiles, there seemed to be a real sense of family unity among them. But on closer scrutiny, these polite well-rehearsed gestures soon began to give way to the realities beneath; that is, the lonely heartache that dwelled inside every one of them. But they were clearly grateful that we had come to visit with so much food, especially the ice cream.

The only boy in the home, around 4 years in age, the younger brother of one of the resident girls, had now been woken up to join us. Immediately he made a dart for me across the room and held onto my trousers. I picked him up and put him to my chest and he clung to me in a way I had never known a child to do before. His clothes were unwashed and reeked of dried urine, but I held him in tight regardless. He was clearly scared of something but had learnt to not show it on his face.

But his intense grip silently told the full story.

It didn't seem like Stella's heart was really in what we were doing. She had been quiet all through the process from first meeting with the social worker the day before through to arriving at the orphanage. Even in the market she seemed a little uninterested in what we were trying to achieve, like some bored teenager trailing behind. I then began to wonder why she had never had children of her own, but it felt too soon to pry. Maybe she was unable to have them for some medical reason.

It was around this time that I began to sense there was something else at work that I couldn't quite put my finger on, and it forced me to start questioning her. I didn't want to know about anything that might rock the hopes and also stability I had to try and sustain for my own sanity. I needed her, because she didn't think I was crazy when I told her what was going on every time I closed my eyes and tried to sleep at night.

As time played out, I realised I had pushed my head through some kind of spiritual membrane and therefore broke through into another realm where I was now open to sheer evil which I had no power to keep off me. These entities now had free reign to do as they pleased, and I couldn't pull my head back through the hole, or close it up for the life of me. Being with Stella at night I thought was a help to me but at the same time I still had to drink each night holding simultaneously onto her in fear that at any given moment I could totally lose my grip on reality. I then began wondering around that same time how many crazed people in the world were really not crazy at all but had actually pushed through into some dark realm like me, and in their despair and panic they ran into the arms of the wrong people to help them. I believed I knew that those same people would have locked me away and injected me also, if I dared to share anything with them.

Maria had stopped sobbing and I wanted to know why, as I nodded to Stella asking her to take the boy from me. She stopped speaking with one of the other girls and came over and took him then I hastily made my way back upstairs towards Maria's room. She was still sat in the same position as before. I gingerly knocked on her door, 'Hola!' I whispered through the gap. She turned. 'Hola' she quietly replied, rubbing her eyes. She looked around 7 years old. I asked if I could enter and sit next to her and she agreed, but then she began to sob again so I tried to comfort her by making fun of myself because my Spanish was so bad. She laughed and this broke the ice.

Her white bedsheets were blackened with grime, although she hadn't slept in them yet, and I couldn't help but notice how neatly she had folded her few pieces of clothing on three crooked wall shelves. She clearly had next to nothing, but what she did own she kept respectfully neat and tidy.

I took a photo out of my wallet and showed her my daughters and she smiled saying how pretty they were. I then decided she at least needed some clean warm bedding and so I said goodbye and would see her soon.

I walked out onto the landing and glanced down through a gap in the steel girded floor and Stella was still holding the young boy. He was laid out flat in her arms and she was swaying him from side to side oddly at her waist height. He, I could see, was enjoying being played with in this way, his free arm dangling in mid flow out to one side. She then glanced up to me and we locked eyes through the same gap in the steel. But something told me the gesture towards the child wasn't real, it was just being played out, it was unmaternal, although she wanted it to appear as such. I didn't want to accept any doubt; I just couldn't afford to, but I still had to keep observing through the gap. It resembled that of the dark watchman, and the entrance to that endless black void outside my uncle's bedroom. It was now manipulating the human body to react in an awkward fashion which in doing then strangely gave itself away, at least enough for me to pick up on anyway. 'So, it isn't that smart', I thought, 'unless perhaps it's just outright cocky and wants me to see'.

I turned from it and made my way back down the fire escape and asked the social worker if she knew anyone with a van so we could go get these kids some warm bedding. She made a call and her friend with a small minibus arrived an hour later and he took us to every market in Cusco until we had purchased 30 sets of bed sheets and the thickest duvets we could find.

They were ecstatic, jumping up and down when we arrived back with the minibus packed full of new warm, clean bedding. We made a human chain once more, bundling them all inside and along up into the first-floor reception room. We said our farewells to a family of genuinely grateful souls. But not before I visited Maria's room one last time and handed her a life size teddy bear to keep her company.

CHAPTER TEN

NEVER ALONE

We spent a further 6 weeks together in the Andes visiting different mountain towns, eating good food, living out a dreamlike existence. We continued to drink the nights away and the orphanage idea slowly became diluted in a sea of booze. It became less important each day, until it finally disappeared. Everything comes to an end, and the time had come where we had to get real, make plans to leave Peru and go our separate ways, at least for a while anyway.

Her plan, however, was to go back and tell her husband that we were an item and that we had spoken about her moving to England once she had filed her divorce. She had no commitments in the US, so once she had wound up her massage business that she had run from home, she would be free to live anywhere in the world. Although my kids were from three different relationships, I had always tried to be equally in all of their lives as much as I could. So, Stella moving to London was going to work better for me because I could still see them regularly and she agreed.

The time came to book our flights to leave Peru. I decided I would walk to a travel agent that I knew offered decent flight deals, but once I left the hotel and was walking through Cusco central out towards the market where the tour operator was situated, I started to feel faint and even had to stop at one point to sit down. It was like I had drifted into a fog and was struggling to think or see straight and my energy felt like it had been completely sapped. I stood up after a while and continued on, wondering if this had something to do with Stella. It dawned on me that we had not been apart at all since she had arrived. It felt like I was trying to shake off some kind of magnetic field as I swayed along the footpath having to consciously take every step with caution in case I veered off onto the road in front of oncoming traffic.

I got to the travel agent and stood outside realising I could not string words together in my mind. How would I be able to sit and choose dates and times, give passport information over and converse in any way with the woman behind the desk? It felt like something was drawing on my brain, attempting to suck it from my skull, my thoughts were being vacuumed away before I could grab hold of any of them. But I decided I would have to at least try and push through because I needed to get booked on a flight home.

I walked into the shop and sat down, managing to explain in a type of drunken slur that I wanted to fly to Lima and then London, but then my vision began to go blurred and cross eyed and I struggled to focus. I could see that her body had turned towards the computer to start searching but I knew I would not be able to make sense to her or be able to complete any transaction. Cold droplets of sweat began to run down my face and I became tremendously aware and paranoid of all the staff like they knew my thoughts. It resembled the psychoses I had struggled with many times in the past, when I had taken too much cocaine and was sure the whole world was watching me suffer, monitoring me live on satellite TV, because I was the subject of some sick global experiment.

My hand went up. 'I...please don't worry, I'll come back, I have something urgent.'

I left the shop, leant against a wall, took out a cigarette and lit it. Then I staggered along the street, back in the direction of the hotel. But as I walked through the square and drew closer to Stella it gradually began to lift and by the time I had reached the room and put the key in the door, this strange heavy pull had completely disappeared. Entering the room, I explained what had just occurred. She said that the same thing had also happened to her and she had had to lie down shortly after I left.

I still had a basic Nokia cell phone, but Stella had purchased her ticket back to Oregon using her iPhone. I asked her to do the same for me because I couldn't go through all that again. We sat and booked my flight and nothing this time tried to prevent me from leaving. I think it was because we were sitting together.

We flew into Lima and then we said our goodbyes. It was difficult for me to let go but we planned to join up again soon; and this was something to look forward to, as long as I could hold out alone and not go mad in the meantime. I didn't know what was going to happen once we parted, although I started to think about seeing my family again back home, wondering how I would explain all the craziness that had taken place over those past few months. I knew it would be almost impossible. Some things I realised I could never repeat for fear of them thinking I had completely lost the plot.

Once we had separated and Stella had gone to her flight gate, it didn't take long before I was reminded I would never walk alone. I strolled into the airport toilet and as I stood at the urinal, I then heard the loud crazed laughter of the Gringo shaman. I quickly looked around expecting to see that he had just walked in, but nobody was there, the room was empty. My heart began to race as I zipped myself up and began searching the cubicles, pushing open the doors one at a time but they were all empty. Two men walked in talking, but neither were him, so I quickly washed my hands and left. I stood outside the entrance to the toilets and scanned the airport but there was no sign of the witchdoctor anywhere.

Arriving back into London I had two immediate options. Head south towards the coast and go back to the trailer where this had all mysteriously started. Or go visit my mother in South London and stay there for a while and catch up with my family.

My mother had been an alcoholic for over thirty years and now lived alone in a two-bed flat, so there was an available spare room. We had had a rocky relationship in the past because we were too much alike and shared the same need to block out the world around us with booze and substances. I had hated staring in the mirror when looking at my mother, it was far too close to home and a reminder of my own damned weaknesses.

Although it was now May and the long winter nights were drawing out, I still had no desire to be alone on that clifftop where so much had gone on. So, I headed for my mother's place and would stay there until Stella flew into London and then we would start looking for a place to live.

So, a week or two stay over at my mother's would be doable.

I was right about not being able to delve into anything; this became even more obvious once I was confronted with the family. I had left in a desperate rush saying very little three months before, genuinely not expecting to return. But now I had returned and was standing in front of them again with knowledge in my head they couldn't possibly begin to understand. I had to protect them from it, which meant keeping it to myself. The only person I could truly confide in was now five thousand miles away on the northwest coast of America.

Even my best friend, Wesley, that I had known since a young boy, who over the years I'd gone through thick and thin with, someone I deeply trusted, the only person who had been able to talk me out of carrying through with so many drug crazed, paranoid, knife wielding, gun toting, insanely violent acts, even he would not get this lunacy that had become my everyday reality. The voice that had been whispering, 'this time you've gone too far' since before leaving for Peru, I was now starting to believe. It had been telling me the truth all along. I just had to try and bury it and hope that it would all eventually go away and leave me alone.

Well, Stella must have got back to Oregon and had second thoughts on the whole plan we had worked out because I got an eagerly awaited call a couple of days after landing at Heathrow telling me she had a good husband right there in the States and she must be crazy wanting to leave him. I couldn't believe my ears. It was as if I was talking to somebody completely different, and I wondered how she could coldly turn on a coin like that. In a way I felt sorry for her husband. She must have talked him into letting her go back out to Peru which meant they must have been together all along and she was playing us both.

I vented my anger at her, someone I thought I knew, but barely did, punching the wall in my mother's living room, making an impression in the plasterboard, cracking the paint inside into a hundred different tiny parts. I told her she should stay there, and it was better I knew now rather than later down the road. Switching off the cell phone, I knocked on my mother's bedroom door and asked her for one of her beers. She was sitting in her usual place in the bed with her dressing gown on, watching TV, drinking.

'Is everything OK?' she sincerely asked, slurring in the far distance behind a fog of tobacco smoke, while at the same time leaning over the side of the bed, drawing the carrier bag full of lager from underneath. She opened it and threw me a can.

'It is what it is', I replied, furious inside at Stella's lies and also wondering what next? But not wanting to explain any further, I decided I would try and knock myself out. 'Got a couple more there?' I asked. She passed me two more and it was already late, so I drank them fast and went to bed.

I don't know what time it was when I awoke in the night laying on my back, my heart beating with anxiety. This was nothing new, except for what was now looking up at me. I felt a presence in the room, as I looked down to my left, I saw a being that resembled a little girl kneeling down on the carpet staring up at me from about three feet away.

It was around the age of 6 and had a roundish face with dark hair swept off its forehead and its eyes were cold, jet black and large, especially wide. I looked away from it as a beam from the headlamps of a passing car shone in through the gaps in the curtains. I turned again to my left and it was still there, even though the room had been illuminated momentarily from the flash of light.

It was expressionless, just staring up at me blankly through those two black holes, as if waiting for me to make a move first. I was now locked into some kind of staring contest, but I was no match and soon froze, breaking eye contact. 'God, please help me' was all I could shakily spit out as I looked away and up to the ceiling.

I was forced to look at it one last time, because it lifted its right hand up covering its mouth, giggling at me from behind like some harmless playful child would, except its laughter was nothing but evil mockery, enjoying, feeding on my fear. It then vanished from my sight.

I lay there for what must have been half an hour until I finally found the guts to lean over and turn on the bedside lamp. I pressed the switch and there was a quick flash and then the bulb blew.

I eventually made my way out to the kitchen to get a glass of water.

As I switched on the living room light, I looked closely at the indent my fist had made earlier in the wall. Something in my stomach turned and a second wave of terror enveloped me, and I began to shudder with cold goose bumps. The mass of tiny cracks inside the imprint had now manifested into the perfect sketch of the same demon that had had possession of Tom in the jungle. The thing that had toyed with me for hours till sunrise in the Amazon was now staring back at me from my mother's wall. I could not have mistaken it, not in a thousand years. I sat down on the sofa and began to struggle to breathe, my heart rushing like crazy. Was I insane or doomed to hell or both? It's like I'd been cursed, bewitched or something worse.

I made it to the bathroom and splashed cold water over my face, frightened to even look up into the mirror for fear of what I might have seen behind me in the room, or even in my own reflection.

I now knew that going to the jungle and taking the potion had failed to heal anything and only helped to seal my fate, leading me further into darkness opening myself up to a realm that wanted me not only dead, but to suffer all the way to the grave. I was clearly in the hands of sheer evil and they were telling me that they could see all my fear and had free reign to toy with me at their own pleasure. I wasn't going to be able to confide in anyone about all of this. Nobody would understand, and every doctor under the sun would write me off as a madman.

I quickly got dressed and packed a bag of clothes. I wouldn't be able to stay there in my mother's place any longer. I couldn't share any of this with her, it just wouldn't be fair. I grabbed my car keys hoping that it would start after sitting unused for three months. I wrote a note to say I had decided to spend some time down on the coast now that the summer was on its way and have some quiet time to think about my next move now Stella wasn't coming. I would call her in a few days.

I quietly left the flat.

The car started first time and I headed for the trailer, but not before calling up my best friend Wesley, apologizing for waking him so early, asking if he could leave a small tub of diazepam out in his garden somewhere, because I was struggling to sleep from jetlag. He said he would put them behind the plant pot near the front door and then was going back to bed as it was only just gone 5am. He asked when we would catch up as he wanted to know how Peru had worked out. I told him I would be in touch, soon enough. I made a detour and grabbed the pills, taking a couple straight away, relaxing shortly after into a pretend bubble of cotton wool while driving down to Peacehaven.

I don't know what I was expecting by going back to the trailer. I walked in and felt the same lonely dark and empty feeling that had accompanied my near demise just a few months before. But at least I didn't have to hopelessly try and explain to anyone what was now going on. I just needed time to work out what I should do next. Whenever I closed my eyes to rest, I was still seeing the reptilian eyes looking back at me, as if they were some kind of fixed part of me, and then also the same vaguely human faces rushing in through the hole the shamans had made in my membrane. But the booze and the diazepam were knocking me out for a few hours at a time and I was managing in this way to get through the nights.

After a few days Stella had got back in touch again and was now staying temporarily with a girlfriend in Portland, Oregon, a massage therapist who also dabbled in the occult. She wanted to use Skype so we could see each other as well as talk and so I dug out a laptop from the wardrobe, happy that I had my confidante back.

Stella had said when we were in Peru that she was open to sex with other women and would consider inviting another woman to share a bed with us as long as she got to pick. I told her I thought we should leave it alone because it would only cause jealousy down the line. I had been sincere about everything I had said in Peru, genuinely wanting to make this thing work between us, but she seemed to have other modern ideas that were beginning to creep in, going on to say how Portland was the new San Francisco, liberal, where anything went. I had sensed all along she'd been trying to lure me into bisexual relations if given half a chance, testing a little at a time.

We made the Skype call and it seemed obvious to me that they had been a little closer than just two student pals that had gone through massage school together. So, once Stella had introduced us and we spoke for a while, her friend then left the room so we could talk privately. She admitted at that point that they had played around a few times and although she hadn't exactly said, I realised I was now expected to go along with this new development if we were to carry on seeing each other. Also, confusingly, she was now going through with the divorce and wanted to come over to London as soon as possible.

Even though the goal posts were being moved around, her telling me this gave me some renewed hope. I was desperate to be in the same room again with the only person on the planet I could talk to about these almost daily occurrences, that to the normal ear were the confessions of a lunatic.

I told her all about the girl at my bedside and the imprint in the wall and that I now felt uneasy in the trailer alone because I was seeing the same dark spirits that had constantly swirled around me each night when I had reached near death, before leaving for Peru. She told me to grind salt in every room because this helped to ward off evil.

It was gone 2am UK time when we had finished our call. I then took the salt and went around the trailer grinding heavily in every room over the furniture and the carpets. The thought of Stella being with her girlfriend thousands of miles away made me feel like a fool and very jealous and I wondered why she would behave in that way. It was as if she wanted me to bow down and worship her in some unhealthy manner and she seemed to lack any sense of loyalty.

I could see it clear enough in my mind, but my heart didn't want to believe that this person who had mirrored me so well inside, saying all the right things, on the other hand could be so cold and emotionally ruthless, pulling the rug from my feet when she pleased. But there was still a hope that things might be different when she arrived, once she was away from whatever attractions were in Portland. I was sure she would like England and then maybe settle down and trust in what we had planned on doing when we were in Peru.

I lay down to rest with the intention of not taking too many pills to crash out. I was thinking of cleaning my act up ready for when she flew in, but after just a few minutes I began to feel anxious and fearful of something in the bedroom. I tried to block it out lying on my side, but I began to get goose bumps and then felt the bedsheet being pulled off my hips slowly from behind and then came the poke in the lower part of my back. 'Get away!' I shouted into the room, more in a cowardly response rather than in a commanding way, jumping up at the same time.

My body was frozen rigid as I clambered out of the bed, clinging onto the door frame without wanting to look behind. In sheer terror I got in the car half-dressed and drove towards my mother's place, all the way thinking that ending my life would be the only way to press the stop button on this horror movie I was permanently trapped inside. I didn't think I was going to be able to hold out for much longer.

CHAPTER ELEVEN

VISION OF JESUS

I tiptoed through the front door of my mother's flat and she was fast asleep in her room. I didn't want to lie down in the bedroom where the devil kid had turned up, so I stretched out on the sofa. It was just gone 4am. In the dark I consciously focused on the welcome ticking of the small carriage clock on the wall cabinet, then I closed my eyes, but as soon as I did the evil faces began to rush me through the hole. I was then forced to open them back up fast, for fear of my mind being stolen. I quickly checked my pockets but found I had left the tub of diazepam in the trailer.

My mum would have booze, she always did, but I didn't want to wake her and have to explain in the middle of the night what I was on the run from. I shut my eyes again but there was no escaping it. How was I supposed to carry on living this way? I had no control over anything anymore. I was just target practise, fodder for demons. I had never given up a fight before, but totally exhausted I closed them once more, this time almost willing them to come, because I had finally had enough.

But then I see Him, sitting relaxed, slightly reclined downwards to my right, in a very humble and lowly position.

It was His side profile He gave me. Head, shoulders and chest and He was clearly speaking something out, into the darkness. He was slim with dark curly hair which was trimmed collar length and His curly black beard was cropped short. He had a prominent nose and looked about thirty in years. He was wearing a cream-coloured tunic, and on His head a crown of thorns. He continued speaking, although nothing audible accompanied the vision. Then all of a sudden everything went completely black and He disappeared.

Opening and closing my eyes at least half a dozen times in quick succession, I soon realised that the hole in my head opened by the shamans had now been closed by the words spoken from the mouth of a man that could have only been Jesus of Nazareth. And now, there was nothing to see but darkness, the way it had always been before I had gone too far and opened myself up to a place I had no business being in. But now the door had been slammed shut in their faces.

I lay there staring up at the ceiling with just the ticking of the carriage clock to remind me I was still there. A tear then ran from both of my eyes, simultaneously down each side of my face, slowly dripping onto the cushion behind my head. I heard them both drop which I strangely took comfort in. I then broke into a smile, whispering a thank you to Jesus for turning up to help. I kept thinking that His words must have been more powerful than the force that had been attacking me through the door for so long. Surely, He is God.

I then must have fallen asleep.

Over the next few days I thought that speaking to the local vicar or priest they simply wouldn't take me seriously, claiming to have been visited by a vision of Jesus, especially with short hair. Every image or statue I had ever seen of Jesus clearly showed he didn't have short hair. How was I to explain this, should I even mention it? I didn't even go to church for a start and never had been other than for funerals, weddings and Sunday school as a very young boy just a couple of times for the chocolate they handed out at the end.

But I remembered how I had got through those nights in the jungle praying in fear to the man on the cross and how I had felt protected from the evil being drummed up. But I still didn't know what to really think. How could I honestly believe that the same God of the Bible from thousands of years ago was now wanting to help me, a criminal from South London with no religious background whatsoever? It just didn't make any sense.

Then again, nothing in the last few months had made any sense to me. I felt sure also, that to start going around telling people Jesus had visited me in the middle of the night speaking words, closing evil doors, would definitely have given people enough reason to write me off as someone that had taken a drug too many, which was true, in the first place, but now it was very different what was happening. It was like some sort of divine fight over my possession.

CHAPTER TWELVE

CALL A PONY

It was a day brighter than most when she walked through the arrivals gate at Heathrow. Summer had fully arrived, and I was looking forward to persuading her to stay the full three months that she had available on her tourist visa. Firstly, so we could enjoy all the good weather together and two, because I was secretly counting all the possible nights I would not have to be alone.

Her divorce had gone through fast without any contesting from her husband. When I eventually got around to telling her the truth about still being married myself, she surprisingly took it well. It wasn't great but she understood and began pushing me to get a divorce so we could move forward, and this I needed to hear.

As we drove out of the airport and connected with the M25 London orbital, I felt something pushing into the back of my driver's seat like the knuckles of a hand. I looked to Stella, but she was just sat there with the window down smoking, taking in her new surroundings, her eyes clearly tired from the long twelve-hour flight from Portland, but she was not anywhere near the rear of my seat. I leant forward away from the seat and then sat back again. After a few seconds the same thing happened; the fingers dug into the small of my back and slowly worked up my spine in a straight line until reaching about level with my chest. I carried on driving, then after about ten minutes it went away.

I decided we should head for the Brands Hatch hotel in the county of Kent. I held a little soft spot for this place because I used to race sports cars on the Brands Hatch circuit situated behind the hotel just a few years before. This going back was a period in my life when I thought I'd found a way to be momentarily free from all my troubles. Once that crash helmet went on, it was just me against myself.

We got booked into the hotel for a few nights. When unpacking her luggage she took out a rock sculpture that stood about 18 inches in height which she had made from beach rocks carefully selected and joined together with a strong resin to create an image of a man and woman intertwined as one. She passed it to me. 'Here this is for you babe, to keep. Do you like it? I thought you should call it "Twin Souls"'.

I did like it, at first.

Creating works of rock art had been something she had done alongside massage therapy, mainly as a hobby, but then she started to receive requests by her clients to create personal figures for them. It took off from there and by all accounts she had been quite successful at it, even putting on a posh gallery exhibition to show her pieces.

After her long journey she soon fell into a deep sleep alongside me. Looking forward to the few good months that lay ahead, feeling very contented, I too, began to doze peacefully. Suddenly I was awoken by the pulling of my hair, as if fingers had grabbed hold of one side and yanked on it. I soon came around again, lying there wondering if this thing would ever be over.

Then what felt like a light feathering across the top of my skull slowly became more narrowed and pressed down until it finally felt as if a sharp fingernail was very slowly being drawn across my scalp from back to front. I brushed the top of my head to make it go away, but after a few moments it started again. I eased out of bed and got dressed, creeping out of the room towards the bar where I swallowed a few shots of tequila and a couple of large brandies to sleep.

The next morning, in the breakfast room, we started talking to a middle-aged couple as we poured coffee at the bar and they invited us to go and sit at their table. They said they owned a small equestrian farm nearby and were there at the hotel celebrating their wedding anniversary.

Once we told them we were looking for a house to rent in the area they offered we go and view a small studio flat they had for rent which was part of the main farmhouse they lived in. They went on to explain that in the upcoming future a two-bedroom barn conversion on the farm would be becoming vacant for rent and we could take that. It looked like things were starting to quickly fall into place.

Once we had moved into the flat, we started helping out with different chores on the farm, Stella in the gardens pruning and planting and I got stuck into helping the resident caretaker dig out a very large fishpond using heavy machinery. We even talked about possibly creating a studio for her in one of the barns so she could carry on with her rock art whilst in England. At times though, I realised she was missing some of her friends back in the

States although she didn't directly say, but I guessed that was to be expected and I just hoped in time that would pass away.

We decided one weekend to travel down to the West Country. One of my daughters lived on the coast of Cornwall. After visiting we then went to stay at the Two Bridges Hotel on Dartmoor National Park. Stella had never spoken much about her early past. All I knew was that she had grown up in Kansas and had moved to Oregon after getting married in her early twenties. During that weekend she began to open up more about her younger life, and surprisingly it unfolded that she had come from a religious background, attending a Christian church regularly each Sunday.

As she shared more about her past, I realised I knew very little about religion. But I did know how real that vision of Jesus had been that night on my mother's couch, and how it made me see that my life would never be the same. And because of it, Stella had even bought me a Holy Bible from a Christian bookstore which I had already started to read each day.

We sat on a low rocky mountain peak studying the rugged beauty of Dartmoor. It was a little breezy, but when it died down, we could almost hear the silence, it was that peaceful and remote. She said how great she thought it would be if Jesus and His disciples were sitting there with us. 'Imagine, that's just how it would have been during the time He walked the earth, teaching the people. Wouldn't it be great, just being in His presence sat here listening to Him preach?' she said. Of course, I agreed, taking in the serenity of the moment and enjoying seeing her open up in that way.

After a while we decided to head back down the hill and once we got to ground level, we sat for a while longer on a slab of rock near the narrow road that snaked through the moors. There was a small herd of moorland ponies grazing just a few hundred yards away. Then right out of the blue, she said excitedly—'let's call in a pony!' I didn't know what she meant exactly so I asked her to explain. 'Let's just sit here, close our eyes and call a pony using the power of our minds. That one at the rear right there,' she said, reaching out her finger and pointing to the one stood at the back of the herd. I agreed and closed my eyes joining in, willing the pony to walk over. About ten seconds later, feeling her glare, I was forced to open mine to find her closely staring at me. She then turned her head toward the herd. My eyes followed. That same pony had now turned and was walking straight towards us and I couldn't quite believe my eyes. The animal strode right over in a straight line without stopping once and stood still about three feet away with its head down and its ears pinned back, unimpressed, even annoyed that it had been led away from the herd, against its will by some invisible force.

I stood up a little freaked out, not expecting the pony to have really done it, then I asked her who she thought was behind it. With a smile, she answered, 'Jesus.' But something inside told me that God had had nothing to do with that stunt, so I said to her, 'Didn't Jesus do miracles to make blind people see and things like that? I don't think He played tricks, that was a trick just for the sake of doing a trick,' but she was adamant she was right, and I was wrong. I reluctantly kept silent, adamant on the other hand that it was an evil spirit that had led the animal over to us. It just felt wrong, the same as when that pendulum stopped in mid flow at a 45-degree angle as I sat on the end of my bed in Cusco. It just felt unkind and loveless.

CHAPTER THIRTEEN

WHO'S JEZEBEL?

The barn became available and we moved in as soon as we could. The rock sculpture of us interlaced found its place on the dining table alongside the Holy Bible that I was now opening more and more each day. I wondered if the answers to all of the crazy things that had been happening were there to be discovered in those ancient texts. I didn't know anything about what the difference was between the Old Testament and the New Testament or how I should even go about reading it, I was completely ignorant, but still it felt good lying open, weighty, in the palms of my hands like I was holding something I should have respect for. 'All of this knowledge must have been written down for some good reason' I thought, with more curiosity each day as I randomly opened it to see what verses of Scripture my eyes fell upon. Frequently I seemed to land in the book of Exodus, a little in from the front of the book, so I thought, maybe I should start by reading this part.

I remembered as a child watching movies about Moses and the story of the Exodus, but it seemed I had been completely unaware of its real meaning. As I continued, I began to see a clear link between what I was reading and what was happening in my own life. It also felt like the text was alive in some way and the more I dug, the more I drew deeper into the spiritual meaning behind the actual historical story. It felt like my eyes were being opened to some kind of an authoritative truth which was also somehow relevant to my own life as I read the words. I really sensed I was being gently told—'FOLLOW ME AND I WILL SET YOU FREE'.

It all began to hit on such a personal note that it could have been written especially for me, it seemed that relevant. I felt compelled to keep reading on in the hope that the path to my healing might be somehow revealed in the scriptures.

During a visit to see my two youngest daughters, the older one passed me a shopping bag with a handful of my old books inside. On the very top sat a little red pocket sized Bible. I picked it up and read what it said on the cover– New Testament & Psalms, and on the inside, my daughter's name was written and dated. 'Don't you need this for school or anything?' I asked her 'No, they gave them out in my last year at Primary, we don't use them now,' she replied.

'Maybe I'm meant to have it,' I wondered, putting it into my inside coat pocket.

It was getting near the time for Stella to return to Portland as her three-month visa had nearly expired. Over that time, we had been making the barn comfortable to live in, although I didn't feel her heart was truly in the bigger plan to settle in England. She had repeatedly said that after being stuck in one place for so long, especially through the winter months, on the dark and rainy coast of Oregon where she had lived with her husband for many years, she definitely didn't want to repeat the same thing again in the cold, wet English countryside.

Then one day in a local country pub she went to use the bathroom and seemed to be taking ages. I decided to go looking for her to check she was OK and found her in the gent's toilet snorting cocaine with some guy she'd never met before. The scene cut through me like a knife as I kicked the door open and pushed the guy up against the wall, dragging her out at the same time. I dragged her through the bar thinking, if she could do it while I was in the same building, how much more back in Portland, thousands of miles away. That same night we argued into the early hours, then I caught her secretly sending messages to a guy in Portland. It was like I was dealing with a complete stranger.

For some time up to that point, I was sure that I'd been seeing her change physical shape. And her voice sounded like it had mutated at times when she had been in Oregon and we were talking over the phone. It was like I was eerily speaking to someone else. The character and tone were not the same woman. She even appeared in certain photos to be extremely younger, even though they had been taken and sent that exact same day. I was sure I'd been witnessing some kind of a demonic shift taking place in her.

Even in the jungle, with Tom the landing strip guy, I'd seen how she couldn't help herself, seeking constant attention from anywhere she could get it. It didn't seem to matter whether it came from a man or woman, as long as she was receiving plenty of it. But it was still a hard thing accepting her heart had no loyalty inside. I guess that other person must have always overpowered her, having the nerve to accuse me of playing around, toying with emotions and coming up with confusing agendas that I constantly struggled to get my head around.

But like a magnet I was still drawn to her, though I realised more and more as time went along, it was something dark that was keeping us together. She would even say often, 'What is this thing going on between us?' like she just wanted it over with too. I knew I did, realizing it would be for the best, but the cruel irony was that my selfish motivation was to keep her close, because I genuinely still believed in some very twisted and distorted way, that she was actually helping my sanity.

It was just a vicious circle.

It was early morning in the barn and the sun had only just risen. I was awoken by a humming noise which at first I thought was a foreign language being spoken by Stella, but then as I fully came around, I realised it was more the sound of something being transmitted through her, and she was playing no part in it. She was fast asleep, her body was turned away from me and her mouth, although not moving, was speaking in a tongue that was not of this world. I lay there with little choice but listen. There were no pauses and no breath was required from her. It was just a continuous monotone which fluctuated only slightly as it projected through her. Surely, it had to be angelic, I thought, then it suddenly stopped. I waited a while to make sure it was over before getting up and putting my dressing gown on and lighting a cigarette.

Stella stayed still in the same position. I glanced across at the rock sculpture of us interlaced, 'twin souls' she had said. Then I looked to the Bible, thinking I needed to open it. I began flicking through the thick wedge of pages, stopping somewhere near the end. I laid it open and my eyes fell on a scripture halfway down the left-hand page. I was reading from the book of Revelation, chapter 2 verse 20, it read—'But I have this against you, that you tolerate that woman Jezebel, who calls herself a prophetess and is teaching and seducing my servants to practise sexual immorality and to eat food sacrificed to idols'. Verse 21 then went on—'I gave her time to repent, but she refuses to repent of her sexual immorality' (ESV).

I slowly closed the Bible and looked down at Stella still fast asleep. 'Who's Jezebel?' I wondered.

Then I remembered that when she had given me a craniosacral head massage a few weeks before, a vision of a woman had appeared very vividly in my mind's eye as Stella pressed on my temples. She was clearly some kind of an ancient, domineering queen that wore an elaborate head dress.

Driving Stella to the airport was still very tough. And watching her disappear through Departures into the busy crowd. I wanted to believe there was at least some part of her which had been sincere all along. Nothing hung around for long, and it seemed everything eventually turned into a lie, falling away to nothing in the end. I needed that unequivocal something to happen and I needed it to happen fast.

Driving back to the farm along the M25 after leaving Heathrow airport, I began feeling the same thing that had happened in Cusco when I left Stella to go and book my flight home. My mind became foggy and I struggled to focus on the road. Something was drawing on my brain like a magnet again, but this time it was accompanied with much more panic and I began to be overwhelmed with fear.

I came off at the next services filled with anxiety, struggling to catch my breath, parking in the nearest space I could find. I couldn't string any thoughts together and this panicked me even further. I turned the engine off and searched around in my coat pockets blindly until I found the little pocket Bible my daughter had given me. 'Jesus!' I cried out in desperation thinking I was having some kind of brain seizure. 'Jesus!!'.

I shakily opened the Bible and landed in the book of Romans. I looked down trying to read the first verse my eyes fell on, struggling to push past the terror, knowing there was power in the words I was holding, forcing myself to focus. I didn't know the passage of text, but I just tried to shout it out into the car anyway. 'For I am convinced that neither death nor life, neither angels nor demons, neither the present nor the future, nor any powers, neither height nor depth, nor anything else in all creation, will be able to separate us from the love of God that is in Christ Jesus our Lord.' (NIV)

I dropped the Bible and held onto the steering wheel, rocking back and forth with my eyes locked tight and began repeating these words, 'Jesus! Nothing can separate your love from me! Jesus! Nothing can separate your love from me! I repeated it over and over until, finally, the fog left me.

It seemed that now Stella and I were separated again I was getting more of the same paralyzing attacks coming, at my mind especially. I bought a small wooden crucifix and hung it on the living room wall in the barn and when I got an incoming assault I would kneel on the floor under the cross and pray, repeating those same precious words that had proven to put a stop to it. 'Jesus! Nothing can separate your love from me!' I would repeat over and over until it fled.

I started to get a repeating nightmare that left me shook up and spun out for the rest of the day. In the dream, I was standing in a remote spot in a woodland, staring at a grassy bank but viewing it as if I could see through the thick mud inside and as I peered in closer, I then readjusted my eyes on what lay in there. It was the dead body of a naked woman. I would then wake up panicking, questioning what was real and what was not, filled with an insane concern of the possibility of it being true. Deep down I knew I was not guilty and therefore could not put a tangible memory to the dream.

Then one day Stella called me and said she had just been given a craniosacral massage by her girlfriend in Portland. 'I was just on the massage table and I had the strangest feeling that you've killed me in another life. I think this whole crazy thing between us is about you now making it up to me'. Then she chuckled, like it was just a joke. But it wasn't funny, because something was trying to persuade me I was paying the price for murdering some woman in a past life. With all that was happening it was hard to not consider the possibility of it being true, but then I would be crippled with dread except for something stronger inside telling me to reject the lie.

Still though, I had to question why this was all happening.

I struggled to be in the barn alone, so I continued to drink heavily and take cocaine and handfuls of diazepam to block out reality, which then led me to watching pornography into the early hours, desperate for a continual sensual expression that would give me a place to hide and be comforted. It seemed my life had taken a full circle and I was now back in the same place I'd been in before leaving for Peru, except now it was even more riddled with darkness.

CHAPTER FOURTEEN

THE GALILEE

I was still selling cocaine on a much smaller scale compared with the past, just keeping a few loyal soldiers in wages that had relied on me for many years to supply their product. But this very familiar environment I once thrived in now became a tremendous burden. Unsurprisingly, I had lost my nerve, the cunning instinct and the boldness it took to survive in that world had long deserted me.

As the saying goes—'I had become a shadow of my former self'. I couldn't see straight, especially down this crooked street, and it was a joke to even think I could still continue in that sphere. I never had it anymore, nor desired it either.

But I still had to collect the thirty grand I was owed before I could throw in the towel and walk away completely. Money was still money and as much as I didn't really need the cash it was still a lot of dough, so I had to push through, meet the guy and pick it up.

I sat at the dinner table of the restaurant with a fellow player I had worked with for many years. He was doing well for himself and wanted to square me up on an old outstanding debt. That was the good news. The bad news was that I sat there feeling as if I really wasn't there at all, like I was beside myself having some kind of an outer body experience or something. I grabbed the holdall of cash from the seat next to me telling him thanks anyway, but I wasn't that hungry and had to be somewhere else on another meet. I staggered out through the door towards the car.

How would I perform out there in the thick of all the lunacy I had grown up in? I simply wouldn't. I was now pathetic and weak. So, shortly after that day, I handed over the last few distribution contacts I had left to the same guy, wanting nothing in return. I had turned my back on a life I couldn't handle anymore. I was now out of the drug game for good.

'Glory to God, through our Lord Jesus Christ...'

It must have been around 5am when I had woken myself up mouthing those words out into the dark living room of the barn. But I had not consciously spoke them, rather I had been awoken by them. I rolled out the sofa bed and lit a cigarette. The more I read the scriptures it became certain there was a war on for my life, so I had to stop playing around and face the facts, and they were facts. Jesus Christ was very real, and demons were very real. I was caught up in the middle of something I didn't understand. But it had become clear, even going right back to the Jungle, every time I called on the name of Jesus Christ, I was then protected from the darkness that been attacking me. I knew He was my only chance.

I realised I only had one move left, and that was to completely run into the full embrace of Jesus' arms, without looking back or stopping once. I read in the Bible that Jesus had been baptised in the river Jordan and I wanted to go there. I sought to be as close to Him as possible. I needed to know if Stella really was on the same side or only in my life to hinder me in some way. I didn't want to think that she could be a part of Satan's plan to destroy me, but I also knew there was something in this wicked spirit of Jezebel which in the Bible had been an arch enemy of God. I truly believed the same spirit had been attacking me through Stella. It was a horrible thought to wonder if Stella knew more than she was letting on and if so, I was now caught up in something even uglier than I first thought. I had always been a fighter and the more I sensed this whole thing was true, the more I then wanted to fight back with the only weapon I realised I had, which was Jesus of Nazareth. I truly believed I had sensed a higher love saying this to my heart all along since I had first read the story of the Exodus.

That same morning, I started to look at flights to Tel Aviv, Israel, waiting expectantly for 3pm to come and Stella to wake up so we could talk around 7am local time in Portland. The phone rang earlier than usual, and she was yelling down the phone, scared stiff. 'Something grabbed me around the throat while I was in the shower! It tried to suffocate me! I couldn't breathe! Babe! I can't stay in this motel another night' she yelled out, hysterically throwing the cell phone onto the bed.

'Stella, listen to me, put the phone back to your ear, I want us to get baptised in Israel, in the Jordan. Will you come with me and get baptised? Listen we need to do this Stella, we need to fight this. Will you come with me?'

The line went quiet as I waited patiently for her reply. I couldn't help but think that as soon as I started looking at flights to Tel Aviv, having made my mind up to go and get baptised, all hell was now breaking loose. I prayed under my breath that Jesus would give her the strength to go through with it.

I could hear her breathing beginning to calm, then she replied. 'OK Tony, let's go and get baptised.'

I smiled inside with the hope that we might be able to fight this and get through it.

'Listen, Stella, how fast can you get here to London? Do you want me to book you a flight straight away?' I said, pushing her to move fast on it. 'OK babe, do what you can, I just need to get out of this motel first, before I'll be able to even think straight, let alone do anything else.'

She arrived in London a few days later and we flew into Tel Aviv on the 20th of June 2016.

I had never been able to bring myself to tell her of my concern that the Jezebel spirit had a powerful hold on her. I didn't really know how to go about it. And whenever I even thought to go there, I became paralyzed with a shortness of breath accompanied with a strong feeling of being intimidated. I just couldn't find the courage to stand up to it, let alone overpower it. I just had to stay quiet for fear of another spiritual attack. But inside I sensed more and more that it just had to be true.

Even on the day we were traveling to Tel Aviv, she wore a revealing blouse and I had to bring to her attention that we were now flying into a religious country where we had to be mindful of what we wore. The strange thing was she had never dressed like that before. Although men were drawn to her like a magnet, it was never because of her wearing seductive clothes, if anything she dressed reasonably, conservatively. So, when she started swaying around Gatwick airport with this provocative blouse on, I couldn't help but think that the spirit of Jezebel was now kicking up about this whole trip to Israel, and our planned baptisms into Christ.

Stella seemed almost drunk and I was having to hold her steady at times, veering through the airport retail outlets searching for a blouse that wouldn't look so jaw dropping when we got to Tel Aviv Arrivals. As the plane took off, I looked forward to downing a few large brandies once the thing levelled up, concerned about what might happen on the banks of the River Jordan.

We hired a car from Tel Aviv airport and headed straight for the sea of Galilee booking a hotel on the shores of Tiberias as Yardenit Baptismal site was just a just short drive south from there, where the sea of Galilee pours from an outlet into the Jordan river.

We obviously didn't know anyone there and weren't sure how it all worked. Some said it was OK for us to just turn up at the baptism site and baptise ourselves, others said that maybe it would be good to try and team up with somebody or a group that were going there and be baptised by their pastor. I thought the latter was a better idea. I wanted to know it had been done properly. Stella was happy to go and jump straight in without a pastor. Again, it all just seemed like fun to her, but I didn't want to take any chances. I had got that far and wanted to be assured I had committed myself fully into the hands of God. I wanted this all to be finally over with. I couldn't do it alone anymore.

The next day we arrived at the baptism site in the hope that somebody would be around to help and sure enough there was a group that had just flown in from Italy and they were all being baptised that same morning. Wearing their white robes, we watched them make their way to the river and then we quickly rented white full-length tunics from the on-site tourist shop, got changed and headed down there to the banks where the last of the group were being dipped under.

I asked the Pastor if we could join them. He looked at me and smiled and I will never forget what I saw in his eyes. I think it must have been Jesus. He radiated with a higher Love and his eyes sparkled with a light that had to be from God. All I remember thinking was that I wanted what he had. The joy I could see and feel flowing through him was immense. A tremendous power was at work and it was overwhelmingly peaceful. I wanted to be in this man's shoes and filled with that same awesome power and love that flowed through him. I had seen a lot in my life and lived many lives, but I knew at that moment what that man had was worth more than all the gold on the planet. I couldn't wait to be dipped under to get some of it.

We walked out into the water chest deep and joined the line—some were laughing, some were crying and some a little bit of both as they dedicated their lives to Jesus, promising to trust in Him and renounce all evil. Stella stood before me in the line and as we neared the Pastor, he asked if I could stand on one side to help support her as she went under. I had been watching her closely and at times she looked a little wobbly, as if she was drunk or stoned so I wondered, even during those last few moments, whether something crazy was going to happen.

I didn't know what I was expecting; nothing could have shocked me anymore. I still thought some kind of last-minute demonic manifestation might occur. I knew I had seen flashes of something dark in her, going right back to Cusco, but I simply didn't want to admit it because I was convinced that I couldn't hack it alone. I just hoped that all the darkness was about to leave us both, so we could have a real fighting chance.

I wasn't sure if I heard her say yes, as the Pastor asked if she acknowledged that Jesus Christ had paid the price for her sins, that His blood shed on the cross cleansed her of every transgression. That was between her and God, I had no say in any of that part. Witnessing that beam of light radiating out of the man right there in front of me, I knew personally that I was in the right place at the right time for once.

It was my turn and she helped the Pastor by holding one side as I agreed to accept Jesus as my Lord and Saviour, promising to repent and to surrender my life to His will. I came up out the water truly hoping that whatever had been toying with me had now been washed away into the Jordan. I even looked back to see if I could see if anything had come out into the water from both of our baptisms, but there was nothing.

We sat on the stone steps by the river taking in the stillness of the moment as the group peacefully dispersed, individually waving goodbye to us. For me so much stood on that day. What would be the outcome I wondered? Had I been set free from the darkness that had plagued my life? Had it worked out in the end and was I finally in the clear?

That same afternoon while Stella was sunbathing down by the pool, I laid down on the bed in our hotel room to try and sleep for the first time since being baptised. It was a moment of truth. For so long inside I had been terrorised and now I could only dare to hope as I shut my eyes that it had all been dealt with, washed away by God. But then disappointingly as I closed my eyes, I was confronted with a beast that I can only describe as being half reptilian, half man, sat in a lofty position wearing a royal crown on its head, defiantly leering down at me almost victoriously.

I sprung open my eyes. How could this be? What was that thing I just saw sniggering down at me?

I went into the bathroom, splashing cold water over my face and looked into the mirror. Drawing even closer still. For crying out loud! What else am I supposed to do?.

I searched for my little red pocket Bible, finding it in my jacket, then I opened the double doors and stepped out onto the first-floor balcony that was just a stone's throw from the water of the Galilee. I opened the Bible, again reading what scripture my eyes first fell upon. It said—'Repent, for the kingdom of God is near you.'

I made my way down to the pool area and ordered myself a large cognac from the terrace bar and stood watching Stella from a distance. A family of four were on holiday. The parents, in their mid-thirties, casually sunbathed whilst their young kids played on a little sandy beach, which was part of the hotel.

I had never been a jealous man in the past, but it was hard with Stella. My acuteness to sniff out trouble seemed to be always working overtime whenever guys were within throwing distance of her. It was as if they fell under her spell and were then hypnotized, even becoming oblivious to their surroundings. In the earlier days it was hard to watch, but as I trusted more in what I was reading from the Bible, it was then that I was able to restrain myself. I sensed I was being helped to understand what was really going on spiritually, behind the scenes. Even so, having strong feelings for a person, that inside her soul the Bible was telling me was as cold as ice and out to destroy me, was a difficult thing to accept, especially when she spoke to my vulnerability so cunningly well.

But it seemed she was doing nothing to provoke any sexual interest herself that afternoon as she lay there almost flat on a sun lounger in a modest bikini donning her large retro sunglasses. I chose to grab my cognac and pull out a chair from under a nearby table to sit in the shade beneath its large umbrella. I then relaxed from a safe distance, enjoying a smoke, looking out over the beautiful sea of Tiberias and the mountains towards the east and Syria.

Like clockwork, every time the man's wife turned her back for a second to pick one of her crying babies up, he was all over Stella like a dog on heat, even though there were other attractive women to choose from that lounged around the pool. 'It's nothing unusual,' I thought, as I swiftly downed my drink, quickly ordering another, looking to abruptly abscond and write the day off. I just wanted to get lost, so I necked the next double just as fast and was now beginning to get fired up as I ordered a third.

I then watched the guy put on a buoyancy aid and walk along a little wooden pontoon and start up one of the handful of jet skis that were bobbing alongside. This made Stella look up to see what the noise was all about. She then spotted me about 50 yards away drinking in the shade. She swung her legs around and stood up, walking my way. 'Hey, watchya doing, Babe?' she lazily asked as she neared, accompanied with those same old relaxed mid-west notes that got me all snagged up in the first place. 'I needed a drink. Why don't you go for a dip in the pool and cool off? You look hot' I replied, starting to feel a welcoming warm embrace from the cognac. 'Do you want a drink?', I asked.

She turned and looked over to the guy on the jet ski getting ready to go out for a run and then replied 'Yeah, maybe in a little while. That looks like a lot of fun. Do think he might let me get on the back and go out with him? I'd like to at least ask the guy, what do think, Babe?'

I was glad she still had on those dark shades because at that moment I had no desire to look into her cruel eyes. It might not have seemed that big of a deal if her intent had been a truly innocent one, but it wasn't innocent. Its motive was to undermine me as a man. Its agenda a very dark and frightening one, which took no prisoners. What was at work inside her was just too ruthless to even begin to contemplate and I wasn't in the mood anymore to try and figure it all out.

But I guess Jezebel, again, had read me like an open book and was about to play me like a well-tuned fiddle once more by challenging my alpha maleness so as to draw me closer into her dark manipulative web. She was a master at stabbing me with her poisoned tail in an already weak and worn-out heart, while at the same time holding me seductively captive, making me believe I'd be in serious danger without her by my side or could even go mad if I dared attempt to walk away from Stella, the vessel she occupied.

I started to see that this entity was on some kind of an assignment to cause real deep hurt, slowly chipping away until I was completely done in, its mandate to spiritually paralyze me and thereby destroy my walk to freedom in Christ. But I was all done with caring for one day. I swallowed my drink, grabbed her hand and without saying a word dragged her through the bar and up the stairs, into the bedroom giving in fully to the jealous lust she had hellishly inflamed inside of me.

CHAPTER FIFTEEN

WHAT'S DELIVERANCE?

A week later we returned to London. Soon after we got back to the farm, I got a call from my sister saying how our mum was in a serious state of depression, drinking a lot more than usual and how she was very worried about her. Stella had already declared she was leaving for Oregon in just a few days, so I called my mother and asked if she would come and stay with me on the farm to have a break from London for a while, as long as she agreed to try and dry out a little. She accepted.

Stella flew back to Portland and I drove to Norbury, South London, to pick up my mum and bring her back to the barn. My mum started to slowly come around, rehydrating and stretching her stomach with a little more food each day until her appetite slowly returned to a reasonable normal and we began to enjoy the quiet time we had together on the farm.

Most days I walked out alone across nearby fields and would often just sit and pray. On the day before she was about to go back home to London, I prayed a certain prayer kneeling in the middle of a meadow. I asked Jesus to put His hand on my mother and take away the alcoholism which had plagued her life for so long. The next day I dropped her back to her London flat.

A week later she called me saying that she was doing really well and—'Guess what, Tone? I haven't had a drink son, since you dropped me back home, not one! And I don't even want one either!', she excitedly exclaimed. This was brilliant news I thought, hearing a refreshing clarity and bounce in her voice but at the same time not really banking on it lasting very long. In the thirty-five years she'd been a serious drinker, on a handful of occasions she had stopped for a week or two at the most, so I thought this was one of those rare strong moments she was experiencing but she then called me a week later and said the same thing and then another week later, still saying that she couldn't even look at booze, let alone put it to her mouth and drink it down.

I never told her that I prayed for her because I didn't think it was important at the time, but as each week passed, I started to seriously wonder if a miracle had really taken place. I was still not sure if I should say anything, so I kept quiet.

I left it three months to be sure before I realised that God had answered my prayer kneeling in that field that day. I then made a visit, sitting down with her and saying I thought a prayer had been answered. She agreed, saying that in those thirty five long agonising, painful years she had never been able to stop drinking in her own strength. 'Yeah! I don't know what's happened son, but I just don't want anything to do with it anymore, it must be a miracle!' she said.

(And as I write these words over four years on, she has never touched a single drop since.)

I couldn't work out why I wasn't getting any better. If anything, the attacks got worse since being baptised. I knew that

Jesus continued to help whenever I called on Him, but why wasn't I getting free from these demonic intrusions in the first place?

Jezebel must have been stepping up her offensive against me, relentlessly in pursuit of my annihilation, using my intimacy with Stella as some kind of a wicked conduit to get to me. I was sure that this evil spirit was luring me into its complex web further, by using Stella as bait to torture and twist me up in jealous knots. But I simply couldn't find the strength to pull away from its grip, untangle myself and run free from its lair. So, like a helpless degraded fool, I would fall for it again and again, punching the wall in rage, drinking myself stupid, then visit a brothel or book into a hotel, to then call a call girl to the room, in the hope she would take me somewhere else, away from all the pain.

'Here, I'm not sure what this is all about, but some fella came up to me in the street earlier today saying he was a Christian and that I needed to give this card to somebody I knew. Not sure what he meant really. What's deliverance?' my mother asked shrugging her shoulders, passing me the small card as she walked past into her kitchen. I started to read what it said, and then a fear erupted inside to the point where I had to go into the bedroom away from my mother. I knew there was some link between the resistance inside and what was written on the card.

It offered Christian deliverance from demons and curses.

I ripped the card up and left without saying a word, strolling to a little grass park I often visited that was positioned on a high point, with a wide view over South London. I realised I was being shown something but was grappling to find the courage to face up to it.

Stella had gone completely off the radar and wasn't answering her cell phone and now she had a new soundtrack on her answerphone—'Give me shelter' by the Rolling Stones, which it directed me to every time I called. So, I guessed she had run away and could now be anywhere in the world.

I stood on that hill looking out over South London thinking that I needed to find a holy place of sanctuary, a bolthole where I could completely switch off from the rest of the world and live quietly for a few weeks or months and be spiritually nursed back to health. Although I felt anxious, I knew I had to look into this deliverance thing and not shun it because of the fear inside.

I decided to look online for anything that felt good to pursue. Within seconds, the first search revealed Ellel Christian Healing and Deliverance Ministry. I clicked, and very nervously began to read on. It was clear they dealt with serious spiritual problems and as I poked around a little more, part of me felt assured I was on the right track but then there was the darker side that shook at my audacity of wanting to get help.

Two weeks before Christmas, after being missing for a month, Stella called me out of the blue crying, saying how she had been a fool and that she missed me and couldn't stomach being apart any longer, saying she wanted to get the first flight over and spend Christmas in the barn, just the two of us. I was glad she had got back in touch and I was looking forward to seeing her again, but by that time I had already decided that I wanted to attend a course which the healing and deliverance ministry ran twice a year. I was looking forward to the prospect of living in the grounds for 3 months solid, receiving regular support by trained ministers and learning what it meant to truly be in the presence of God and to be healed by the love of Christ. But I still had four months until the course actually started in the following April so all I could really do was keep reading the Bible each day and crying out to Jesus whenever the assaults came.

But I had by now learned to live with the pokes in my ribs and the feeling of being held down and suffocated in the middle of the night. The manifestation of the fingernail drawn slowly across my scalp still continued daily, and then of course those snake eyes had been a constant internal fixture since the night of the Gringo shaman's ceremony almost three years before.

Stella flew into London a week before Christmas and I rushed out to buy a tree and decorations for the barn and we stocked up with plenty of food to see us through the festive season. As I began explaining all about this Christian ministry I had been in touch with, she seemed to show interest browsing their website, saying she would even consider going on this course herself. We even attended the local village church together on Christmas Eve, promising each other as we strolled back along the dark lane towards the farm after the midnight service, 'We should fight this thing through to the end.' But we realised that for both of us to enrol on that 3 months course together, we would need to be married before we could enter as a couple.

In between Christmas and New Year, I visited the local historic town of West Malling alone, just a few miles from the farm. I wandered along the chilly main street, heartily warmed under the glimmer of the Christmas lights and the chimes of the distant church bells, observing the stir of families, enjoying the hum of goodwill. Wrapped up snug with my hands in my coat pockets, I glanced across the wet cobbled street to an old, antique jewellers with its flickering window display conveying a warm message to 'come in and take a look'. I strolled across, entered the little shop and carefully chose her engagement ring.

One night we decided to go online and view some of the Ellel Ministries online sermons. There was a long list to choose from and as we sat on the sofa browsing down the list, I saw one named Identifying Jezebel. Still apprehensive, I just said—'You can choose which one, I'm easy.'

Amazingly she then moved the cursor to the same one and clicked. I sat waiting for it to begin.

It was a very powerful message being preached and everything the man was saying aligned with my own experience of seeing first-hand how this entity seemed to manipulate its host and whoever the host was spiritually in proximity to. About 20 minutes into the Seminar she began to get very restless, then all of a sudden passed the laptop over to me. She stood up holding her stomach saying. 'I feel like crap, that must have something to do with me. Look, I've come over all clammy and I feel sick!', she said, wiping the cold moisture away from her forehead.

I closed the computer down thinking, 'This is the time for her eyes to be opened to what's really been going on' as she swayed back and forth across the room, her breathing all irregular.

'Stella, listen, sit down, we need to talk about this… What we've just heard him talking about, I've seen at work, going almost right back to the very beginning, when we first met, but listen, we can beat this if we work together on it'. I reached out my hand and took hers, 'We should get married as soon as possible and then enrol on that course together and I believe God will do the rest for us.'

She then snatched her hand away and jumped-up shouting, 'I will never back down to a man! Neither will I be ruled by any man! Never! Do you hear me? Never!', she screamed... She then grabbed her coat on the way out. I stood at the window watching her get smaller and smaller until she finally disappeared out of sight along a bridle path that ran through the field opposite the farm into woods far in the distance. After a while she returned much calmer, saying there was something in all this.

CHAPTER SIXTEEN

I HOPE YOUR PLANE CRASHES

We agreed that the only way we would be able to get married in time for the April start date would be if we did it in the US where there were a lot less hurdles to jump over compared with England.

As long as we had a valid certificate to confirm we had been married before God then we would be legal to enter the ministry as a couple and that was all we were told we needed. Stella made a call to a friend that had a relation who was a pastor in Oregon. He responded to our email and within two days we had booked a date with him to marry us in just three weeks on a little rocky beach somewhere. She contacted her mother and stepfather in Kansas, asking her stepdad if he would give her away on the day and he agreed, so it was arranged they would fly out to Portland to bless and witness our future marriage. A week later we flew into Portland to get prepared.

Stella had been renting a nice roomy house. The place had plenty of living space worked out over two floors and she had been using the downstairs for her massage therapy work. For this weekend her parents would occupy the whole downstairs and we would use the upstairs. Her parents were Christian people and I thought it was a good thing that they were coming out to bless us, but then Stella started to behave peculiarly as if wrestling with something inside.

A couple of days before her parents were due to fly into Portland, I sat watching TV in the open plan kitchen and lounge area while Stella prepared a meal. I just happened to look over as she walked from one end of the kitchen bar to the other. What I saw next I would never forget. I was witnessing another demon manifest.

She wobbled, frail on her feet, slightly bent over like her life blood had been drained out. Her facial skin was so wrinkled and withered that a person could never have reached those years in age. She was gawking downwards, unfocused and her eyes appeared glazed over as if she had severe cataracts, her pupils almost hidden behind a white film. Her body looked all shrunken, mummified almost, as she slowly shuffled her feet along, seemingly too weak to lift them up.

I don't know how much of the real Stella was left, I couldn't have calculated that, but it was clear she'd been completely defiled and what remained was just a fraction, a hollow shell, the rest having been given over to the devil. I grabbed her car keys and left.

I stood on the shore of the Colombia river that afternoon not knowing what to do. It was now clear she had a demon. Entering that deliverance ministry had to be our only hope if we were to survive this. Desperately wanting to hide from the storm, smoking one cigarette after another, I stood watching barges and larger ships ferry past but I was in no rush to go back to the house.

I looked along the shoreline and noticed a waterside bar, but this wasn't going to disappear in a river of booze. I couldn't bury my head in the sand and hide from this one. All I could hope for was that if we entered that healing ministry, God would pull us through this thing and out the other side.

I walked back into the house a few hours later and found her drunk out of her brains, questioning where I'd been all afternoon, accusing me of trying to pick up the girl that worked in the bar down on the fishing marina. I told her I'd been nowhere near the place.

'Why do you wanna marry me anyhow? You could get yaself some young meat like her. So why me hey? Here, take a drink Babe, come on, get drunk with me', she slurred, pouring me out a large glass of red wine, which I thought I was going to end up wearing, but she passed it to me instead.

'Listen, you are serious, right, about going into this deliverance ministry?' I asked, needing assurance but secretly wanting her to say no so I could give myself an excuse to head straight for the airport. I now had serious doubts about the whole thing, especially if she refused any help down the line. Where would that leave me then? I kept thinking. I couldn't make her go into that place, I realised.

I told her I was going out into the yard to cut some wood for the fire, but she continued to sling drunken abuse at me. Then I decided I had just about had enough, pushing past her into the bedroom snatching my passport from the bedside table, making my way back out towards the front door. 'I'm going to the Sheraton', I said as calmly as I could, but she continued to holler and swear. I gripped her around the throat and pinned her down into the armchair shouting back at her—'Listen to me! Get well! Do hear me, get well Stella! You're very sick, get well woman!'

I left her there loud and drunk.

I called a taxi to take me to the Sheraton Hotel near Portland airport, and booked myself a room there. She didn't call me once that night and so I assumed she'd passed out cold and slept right through. Once I was in the room, I used the hotel phone and booked myself on a flight back to London which was leaving early afternoon the following day. I then sent Stella a text telling her that I was sorry, but I was booked on a flight and going. I then finally laid my head down to rest.

I awoke sometime in the middle of the night. I got up and switched the bathroom light on, to take a leak. As I walked in and glanced into the mirror, in shock, I found something else glaring back at me. It was partly me, but partly reptilian, like some kind of demonic hologram inside me.

How much more proof did I need? I was clearly very sick and needed help.

An hour or so after first light I watched her through the bedroom window drive into the hotel carpark. She got out of the car and walked towards the entrance pulling my small suitcase of clothes behind her. We sat in the downstairs bar lounge together and she insisted her parents were coming and we should go through with the marriage and cancel my flight. I still couldn't bring myself to try and explain what I had seen in her the day before. How could I? Where would I start? And also, what I had seen sneering back at me in the mirror, just a few hours before? I'd perceived too much and I didn't know which way to turn anymore. She stood up holding her hand out asking me to take her upstairs and like a moth to candlelight, I took a hold of it and walked her to the room.

After we'd been together, she started to get dressed, saying she was going for a smoke downstairs, still insisting I stay on, but I told her that she should go into the deliverance ministry alone and I would wait there in London for her to finish the retreat. Then maybe I could go in after her separately. It had already been three years, so I thought I could probably wait another few more months. Well, she began shouting again, saying that she would never have gone into that stupid place anyway. As she held the door open to leave, she took her ring off and threw it at me, and then started walking out. 'I hope your plane crashes'.

I stood at the window and watched her march back to the car, get in and drive away.

CHAPTER SEVENTEEN

AND WHAT IS CRAZY?

I returned to the barn and being away from Stella as usual brought more demonic attacks, and I found myself on my knees pleading to Jesus to stop them. After a few weeks she unexpectedly contacted me, saying that she wanted to apply to go on the Ministry course which we'd been planning all along, but never thinking to apologize for cursing my flight back to London, on that last morning.

I'd already applied to enter on the same date and had been accepted but agreed with Stella to hold back and allow her to go first as it wouldn't be a great idea for us both to be in this place together. It would be just too complicated. She agreed to go in alone and I would apply on the following start date in the upcoming October. In the meantime, I would visit her there at weekends and speak on the phone.

But as the time neared the start date of the course, she refused to answer her cell phone and I was getting even worse attacks. I wasn't sure if she'd been lying all along and had never applied in the first place. I called the ministry, desperate for an answer, but they said they were sorry but that they couldn't give that kind of information out as we were not married. I was no further forward.

One night under constant attack, on my knees before the cross, I looked up at the rock sculpture that still stood on the dining table and a wave of insight washed over me, as if I was seeing into the spirit world, and just knew I had to get rid of it. I could clearly see that all along it had represented an evil entanglement between Stella and me, and that Jezebel was merged within it. I grabbed hold of the thing and ran downstairs into the night, slamming it frenziedly into the ground, picking up each broken part, pelting it to the concrete, smashing them into smaller pieces.

Had she been playing me all along, having already given herself up to the will of Satan, and was I now caught up in her web of evil? And just like this dammed sculpture she'd made, I was clearly being shown we were now one flesh, spiritually joined and interwoven.

I ran back inside, realising I had to get disconnected from her completely. Bagging her clothes, going along all the shelves, even removing every pebble she had kept from those country walks, I said to myself, 'She's using these as evil conduits to keep me further bewitched.', tipping them all into the bin liner with all the rest of her stuff.

I slung it all into the boot of the car along with every broken part of the sculpture and headed out to the nearest recycling point. I tipped all the rocks onto the ground then shoved her clothes through the hole in the bin. I then searched the car, finding small rocks that she'd placed inside the passenger's door panel, the glove box and every other storage pocket that I opened. It was their energy she was so fascinated with she had always said, eyes momentarily eclipsed.

I cast them into the nearby field as hard as I could.

The next day I drove back to the town of West Malling and again stood in the High Street across from the jewellers holding the only thing left of her in my right hand. 'Should I just sell it back to them cheap?' I thought, but then I glanced up and down the street looking for another option that might bring some good instead. There was a charity shop just a few doors along that supported people with mental health problems.

As much as I knew I wasn't crazy, I did know what it felt like to be helplessly alone, caught up against my will inside a foreign and hostile realm where the dwellers held no mercy for my well-being. A domain that few truly knew existed at all. I then wondered again, how many people were really not mad but instead under siege from the kingdom of darkness. And what is crazy? Perhaps there's no such thing, only demonic infiltration, I thought. Having no doubt in my mind, the demonic was the real cause of mental illness.

I headed for the door anyway, but not before first praying, asking Jesus to break any curse that may have been connected to Stella's evil infested soul, before it's then passed on and worn by another.

I entered the charity shop and handed it to the lady behind the counter, showing her the original receipt that was folded neatly in the bottom of the box, for proof of ownership. I then went on to explain that I had bought it from the jewellers just across the street, but that my situation had now changed. With her eyes politely down, she insisted I take a receipt, although I didn't want one, but she pressed that I should, accompanied with a glow of appreciation and a little compassion. I waited the minute it took for her to write one out, then left the shop ripping it up as I walked along the street, discarding the pieces into a nearby waste bin.

CHAPTER EIGHTEEN

PLEASE, SET ME FREE

I had missed the April start date to enter into Ellel ministry, because of all the confusion Stella had created by saying she was going there and then disappearing off the face of the earth. She had even changed her answerphone soundtrack to some heavy metal, head banging number, which she had never shown any interest in before. But I guessed she was coming alongside her next victim, mimicking his interests, mirroring his inner dreams. She was mutating once more in order to snare the next one for her jailer, the evil spirit of Queen Jezebel and ultimately Satan himself.

Three months later, I finally limped into Ellel Pierrepont, the Christian healing and deliverance ministry's spiritual centre, which is housed in an old converted Manor house, situated on a small country estate in the south of England. I was attending a nine-day biblical teaching and healing retreat, with on call prayer ministers to help with my spiritual needs as the war inside of me began to fully erupt.

The Bible says—'There is a time for everything', and I realised at this very moment in my life I was being called to know the truth, the very truth, the Bible says—'will make you free'.

And finally, I could see, it was indeed my time to now take that unequivocal step, the one I had wanted to take nearly all my life, to never look back in doubt at the decision I had made. It was time to burn all bridges that led to evil, once and for all. Never ever could I have imagined though that this renewing, this rebirth I had always dreamed of, would have presented itself in the knowledge that it did.

It would be the beginning of a hard and long battle, and it would mean for me to truly lay down what was left of my broken life in order that I receive the life Jesus had for me and thereby win the battle that had been raging over my soul. Not just for those last three torturous years, but in fact my whole life I'd been in the trenches, in a spiritual war, being constantly bombarded with enemy fire, but not knowing how to fight back myself. Now this was all about to change.

I had finally made it to a holy sanctuary where there were courageous, but gentle, godly people that understood the horror I had been living through and were willing to get in the trenches alongside me. And more importantly, teach me how to use the authority I had as a true follower of Jesus Christ to overcome the kingdom of darkness which had had its cruel way with me for far, far too long.

Jesus had conquered all evil, and He had suffered for all my sins, paying the penalty for them on the cross, doing so by a tremendous act of divine love, so that I would be set free, and have life abundantly through Him, if I chose to accept it from Him. But in order for me to receive the full healing that Jesus had for me, there was something I had to do first, myself.

When I had been baptized in the river Jordan in Israel, before I went under the surface I had promised to repent. But this repentance part went in one ear and straight out the other. I'd never been taught what true repentance meant, to be truly sorrowful for my sins before God and how important that heart condition was to my healing and deliverance in Christ. It is written in the book of Matthew that Jesus' very first word He spoke when He first began to teach was this, 'REPENT', then He went on to say in the same sentence, 'because the kingdom of God is near you' meaning Himself.

There was a large wooden cross that stood on the grounds of Ellel Pierrepont, and on the last day of the retreat I went and knelt before it, quietly alone. The devil had been putting up a fierce resistance all morning, attempting to make me back out. He didn't want me to be truly repentant of anything. He didn't want me to hand Jesus Christ of Nazareth legal authority to deliver me from the sins the devil held me locked up in prison over. He didn't want me to know the truth and to be truly forgiven for every evil act I had ever done and therefore be eternally set free. Satan most definitely didn't want that to happen, because he would then lose his grip on me, not just in this life, but for ever.

Jesus—and the Kingdom of God had come near me and I was required by divine, legal law to repent before Him so that I may then have my prison gate opened and walk free from eternal condemnation.

Satan did not want me to repent, but I had now been educated on this biblical truth and had grasped the huge, life giving, healing potential this handover of divine authority would have over my whole life. I had learned that at the very centre of this fight was my God given gift of free will, and its willingness, or not, to surrender fully to the will of Jesus

Christ would determine the outcome of each individual battle and ultimately the whole war that raged over my soul. The evil inside was now bent on making me feel tremendously fearful to push through with truly repenting, in the foreknowledge that its time would be up, and therefore would have to leave as a consequence.

In this understanding, I prayed out loud, with all my heart—'Lord Jesus! Please—please forgive me for all the evil I have ever done. I truly repent and I make you Lord and Saviour over all of my life. Jesus Christ of Nazareth, I surrender my life to You. Please, set me free'

The following day was a Saturday and the ministry held a public event which was known as Jesus Heals day. People arrived from all over to hear some Biblical teaching and then receive healing and deliverance prayers, if they chose to, by trained ministers that sat in pairs around the edge of the packed hall. Once the teaching had finished, we were asked to make a single line along the centre of the hall in preparation for each to be allocated our prayer team. I then began to feel a lot of fear, and my vision went strange as if sections of the hall had vanished.

I headed for the exit doors to escape, but my legs felt like they were jelly underneath me and therefore I had to be mindful of every step going forward. I then realised that all sounds were beginning to echo as well, as if I was hearing them from the far end of a tunnel. Something was seriously wrong.

As I headed for the exit doors, one of the ministers, a woman who had prayed with me earlier in the week whilst sitting on a little wooden bench down by the river, reached out—'Tony, are you OK? You should really go up for prayer now', she said, her words all distorted. I nodded, trying to put on a brave face not wanting to show my confusion, while at the same time feeling the clamminess building on my face and the red glow which must have been an outward response to the extreme fight that had kicked off inside. I shuffled towards the queue, through the frightening crowd, like a delirious lost child with a dangerously high temperature.

On the stage were two middle-aged men, one casually dressed in a tracksuit and the other wearing a more formal, shirt and trousers. They were sat on two chairs with an empty one opposite them. The lady stood at the front that was directing the people to the various prayer teams sent me in their direction, telling me to take the third seat. The more casual one I had met; he was just completing a year-long ministry course. He was a pleasant Irishman who I'd shared a lunch table with earlier in the week, but the smarter guy I hadn't seen before. They met me with reassuring smiles, tenderly asking me what I needed deliverance from in my life. The list was long....

Other than all the obvious vices I'd been willingly caught up in my whole life. I had also read in the Bible during that past week that my grandparents' involvement with the Ouija board and other occult practises, coupled with my own involvement throughout my life during desperate times, such as visiting tarot card/palm readers and clairvoyants, had opened me up tremendously to the demonic, giving Satan right of entry into my life.

The Bible says that Satan comes to steal and to kill and to destroy us. This means our children and our children's children also. One way he is able to keep us in spiritual prison is through the occult sins of our close ancestors. The curses derived from these practices of witchcraft then carry down through the family lines to the third and fourth generations, even as far as ten generations for sexual sins.

As I sat and learned about all what the Bible said about all this, it made so much sense to me and suggested why I had never been able to succeed in anything truly good in my life. Instead, little by little, my life got darker and lonelier instead of brighter and more fulfilled, until finally I fell into severe depression where I nearly ended it all. It was clear to me there was a link. God's first commandment to us is, "You shall have no other gods before Me". I had much to forgive my ancestors for.

I had read in the Bible that as followers of Christ we should, 'Confess your sins to one another, and pray for one another, that you may be healed.' (James 5:16 RSV). I chose to confess and repent before those two brothers in Christ, because they stood as legal witnesses before God that I was now bringing out into the light my involvement in witchcraft during my time in the jungle and also throughout my whole drug taking life, because I had now learned from the Bible that all drug taking in God's sight is rebellion, which is as the same as witchcraft, which had seriously opened me up to the demonic before even going to the jungle.

Once I had confessed and repented, asking Jesus to forgive me, the guy wearing the shirt and trousers reached out his hand, hovering his open palm just above the back of my neck and then he began praying in a strange language which I had recently learned was the practise of praying in tongues. Then the Irishman began to pray in the same way with his open hand reached out as if projecting God's will towards me.

I then sensed something move which felt coiled at the bottom of my spine spring upwards, unravelling vertically. I jolted forward and discharged an unexpected grunt as the demon headed for the way out, which seemed to be through the back of my neck. My head jolted simultaneously along with every coil that released, until the whole serpent had been completely expelled from my body.

The thing that had entered me during the Gringo ceremony three years previously had left. That very same reptilian spirit I had seen sneering back at me in the mirror of the Sheraton Hotel, the one that had mocked me just hours after being baptised from a lofty height, wearing a royal crown, boldly stating it was still lord over my life was finally gone. Why did it not go before? Because my heart had not yet repented and therefore the demon had a legal right to be there. But now that same demon had been cast out, in just a few seconds, by the power of the Holy Spirit.

I stood up, stunned by the reality of what had just been evicted from me, but at the same time welcoming the clarity, the sense of freedom that was now overwhelming me. I simply said thank you to the two ministers, nothing more, still in a daze, then walked off the stage and through the busy hall out into the daylight. Striding with a spring in my step into a nearby field, holding my hands up skywards in total amazement, I thanked Jesus for what He had just done for me.

The demon spirit had been driven out, expelled from me. Jesus had demonstrated the freedom that comes from true repentance in Him. He is God and there is no other.

The Bible says, 'Therefore God also has highly exalted Him and given Him the name which is above every name, that at the name of Jesus every knee should bow, of those in heaven, and of those on the earth, and of those under the earth, and that every tongue should confess that Jesus Christ is Lord, to the glory of God the father.' (Philippians 2:9-11 RSV).

I realised on that day, a very precious divine law, which is— that Godly sorrow, true repentance and honest confession before the feet of Jesus Christ of Nazareth would hold the key to my full healing and deliverance, from the damning consequences of a life so wrongly lived.

"And you shall know the truth,
and the truth shall make you free."
(John 8:32 RSV)

IF A WICKED MAN
John Sealey

The True Crime Biography of John Lawson, born in Scotland and raised in South Africa until the age of ten, where his policeman father locked him home alone and never returned. Rescued after four days without food, he was sent back to Scotland where rage grew inside him. In Glasgow, Liverpool, Manchester, and London's Soho, his fighting skills and courage made him a man with a reputation. Riding with a biker gang, trained as a bodyguard, and graduating to "debt collecting" for international racketeers, his life was full of brutality and crime. It was only when serving his third jail sentence, he found the way to escape the prison of brutality that his life had become. A remarkable story of one man's escape from his past life by finding the truth that set him free.

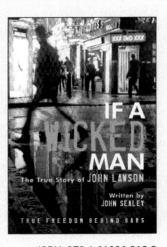

ISBN: 978-1-61036-212-2

SEARCH N RESCUE
Eddie Roman

Search N Rescue is a practical guide to reaching people with the good news of Jesus Christ. Eddie has been teaching evangelism classes and leading outreaches for the past six years. As producer/director of Ray Comfort and Kirk Cameron's TV show, The Way of the Master, Eddie knows how to communicate deep truths in a way that is easy to grasp. Many Christians want to share the gospel with friends and family, but few actually do. Fear of rejection stifles many. Others don't share Christ because they don't know what to say. Drawing insight from the Bible as well as personal experience, Eddie gives clear instruction on how to overcome the obstacles and share your faith..

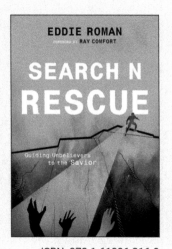

eddieroman.com

ISBN: 978-1-61036-216-0

BEAUTY FROM ASHES
Donna Sparks

In a transparent and powerful manner, the author reveals how the Lord took her from the ashes of a life devastated by failed relationships and destructive behavior to bring her into a beautiful and powerful relationship with Him. The author encourages others to allow the Lord to do the same for them.

Donna Sparks is an Assemblies of God evangelist who travels widely to speak at women's conferences and retreats. She lives in Tennessee.

www.story-of-grace.com

www.facebook.com/
  donnasparksministries/

www.facebook.com/
  AuthorDonnaSparks/

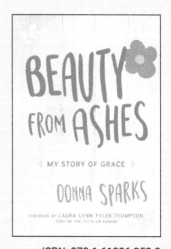

ISBN: 978-1-61036-252-8

YOUR FIRST STEP TO FREEDOM
Don Wilkerson

This instructional and informative book is written for those who want to help someone that is struggling with an addiction. For those struggling with a life-controlling problem, for church leaders, youth ministers, families, and friends of an addict, this book has been written for you.

With over 50 years of experience and seeing firsthand that people do not know how to help those suffering with an addiction, Don Wilkerson has written this book to help. Find useful guidance on:

- Taking the first step toward freedom
- Ministering to families of addicts
- Steps toward intervention for loved ones
- How to avoid a relapse
- From denial to decision
- And much more

ISBN: 978-1-61036-214-6

BRIDGE LOGOS

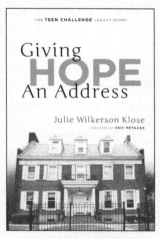